In Praise of H
A Journey from Intuition to Innovation and Beyond

When the person who has interviewed over 625 (and growing) authors, thought leaders, and experts writes a book, I'm fascinated to read it. *Hacking the Gap* is both a book and important model for closing that void between where we are and where we would like to be. By sprinkling personal stories along with pearls of wisdom in an easy-reading style, *Hacking the Gap* will fill what's missing in your life.

–Kevin W. McCarthy, author of *The On-Purpose Person* and *The On-Purpose Business Person*

Hacking the Gap is a masterwork of wisdom and practical advice for success in Life and Business. Author Greg Voisen has amassed a lifetime of experiences, good and bad, that can save readers a lot of pain and time. A great read!

–Michael McCafferty, serial entrepreneur, inventor of CRM software

I believe that happiness is the enjoyment of the pursuit of your potential and *Hacking the Gap* provides a great strategy in order to help you along the way as you pursue your goals.

–David Meltzer CEO, Sports 1 Marketing, author of *Connected to Goodness: Manifest Everything You Desire in Business and Life*

I think Greg Voisen is brilliant. This is a man who has lived and studied his message above and beyond, and it's evident in this fantastic book. Intuition and innovation will soon be two of the most sought after capacities at work and home and this book will help you access and magnify those gifts—experience the magic of life.

–Jonathan H. Ellerby PhD, best-selling author of *Inspiration Deficit Disorder*

Hacking the Gap takes the reader on a journey through the creative process. Tapping into our intuition and learning how to follow through on your great ideas is a powerful process. Listening to the inner voice for guidance regarding the development of your great ideas is certainly worth learning how to fine tune—and *Hacking the Gap* does just that. Let Greg Voisen be your guide, you will grow both professionally and personally and you will be glad you took the journey.

—Bo Parfet, author of *Die Trying: One Man's Quest to Conquer the Seven Summits*

It takes courage to be a "frontrunner" in any field; passion to persist against the stream of convention; to prevail, it takes wisdom. Greg Voisen is a frontrunner: passionate, courageous, and wise.

—Guy Finley, best-selling author of *The Secret of Letting Go*

Most entrepreneurs don't cross the gap between creative, hard working visionaries to clear, consummate effective business professionals. Greg Voisen has...and this book will show you how you too can tune in, tap into and turn on your intuitive genius and then leverage it into inspired action and results. I'm a big fan of high vibration thinking applied to practical action, and Greg's model is the best I've seen.

—David M. Corbin, author of *Preventing BrandSlaughter* and *Illuminate: Harnessing The Positive Power of Negative Thinking*

Greg Voisen has distilled his decades of business acumen into an entertaining, easy-to-read manual for success in business and perhaps everyday life. *Hacking the Gap* provides a step-by-step path to creating what you really want in life, and the book has great illustrations to remind the reader of salient points. It's just what we need today when we don't have enough time to read a lengthy volume or learn from all the successes and mistakes Greg has made over the years.

—L. Steven Sieden, author of *Buckminster Fuller's Universe* and *A Fuller View, Buckminster Fuller's Vision of Hope and Abundance for All*

Greg Voisen's new book—*Hacking the Gap*—is for any entrepreneur or business person who wants to benefit from his years of study and focus on personal growth and business. He has hundreds of hours of interviews with thought leaders and authors at his podcast program Inside Personal Growth. Combined with his own personal experiences as a serial entrepreneur, this book makes Greg the "go-to" person for taking your product or service from the spark of your intuition to making the idea a successful venture. *Hacking the Gap* is a must read if you are trying to bring any new product to market or reinvent your organization.

—Don Green, Executive Director of Napoleon Hill Foundation, author of *Everything I Know About Success I Learned from Napoleon Hill: Essential Lessons for Using the Power of Positive Thinking*

Hacking the Gap is a unique, personal and jam-packed reflection on Greg Voisen's 40-year journey that blends business, entrepreneurship, and personal growth. While you might be able to consume its eight chapters in a couple of hours, allow yourself plenty of moments to highlight the standout nuggets from among the hundreds he offers—in addition to the collection of actionable measures listed as "Mindset Applications" at the end of each chapter. After interviewing hundreds of authors of personal growth books, Greg has written a Ph.D. dissertation of an overview on the subject of harnessing one's potential. The book also triggered my imagination, conjuring up the printed version of an extended John Cage symphony built on a river of practical ideas and practices.

If you've ever struggled with the initiation of a big project, just heeding his chapter on incubation and the need to take a step back, might enable you to make more headway (with fewer mistakes) than you could have imagined without doing so. I found his selected quotations and original illustrations to be juicy additions to a rich tapestry of ideas, stories and perspectives. All in all, after spending time in each of its chapters, I learned a lot (like the four disciplines of execution developed by Clayton Christensen,) and came away with a much better sense of what I've missed doing in the past, and what I need to do in the future. I will dip into this well again.

—David Winkelman, author of *Embracing Change from the Inside Out*

Greg's magic lies in his extraordinary ability to manifest, interview, and write—he's a guy who knows how to get things done, listen intensely to others, and share his vast insights and experience in compelling stories. You get all that in *Hacking the Gap*—it's inspirational and instructional; it provides a roadmap, highlights must-see stops, and spells out tools to make the most of the journey. If you're on a quest to realize the best in you, your ideas, and people around you, then this is a must read. And Greg has invested his considerable talents to write a compelling and intelligent read you'll want to absorb deeply.

—Eric Kaufmann, author of *The Four Virtues of a Leader*,
President of Sagatica—an Executive Development Consultancy

Hacking the Gap is an excellent read, chronicling the challenges and breakthroughs of a serial entrepreneur. In an intriguing format, Greg Voisen has been able to weave his personal story into the broader universal challenge of growing, learning and applying key skills he's learned along his journey. *Hacking the Gap* will help the reader understand and learn from Greg's adventures and even his mistakes. This book is designed to seriously transform your life in fulfilling, rewarding and purposeful directions. I've been Greg's friend and colleague for years now, and am pleased that he's finally written this valuable book to spread his landmark insights and breakthroughs to a wide entrepreneurial audience.

—John Selby, author of *Quiet Your Mind: An Easy-To-Use Guide to Ending Chronic Worry and Negative Thoughts and Living a Calmer Life*

Greg's great new book provides a practical step-by-step process for finding fulfillment through living the life your soul intended for you.

—Richard Barrett, founder and chairman of the Barrett Values Centre,
author of *A New Psychology of Human Well-Being*

Tapping into the power of intuition is one of the most important skills for anyone interested in living a better, more fulfilling, life. And yet it is also one of the least understood. Greg Voisen's *Hacking the Gap* offers an essential user manual for anyone seeking to enhance their ability to innovate, work in flow, and live a more meaningful life.

—Nate Klemp, PhD, Co-Founder and Chief Innovation Officer at
LIFE Cross Training, author of the *New York Times* best-selling book
Start Here: Master the Lifelong Habit of Wellbeing

Hacking the Gap is a book that will bring out the best in any inventor, entrepreneur or agent for social change. It guides the reader through the challenges of bringing a product or service to market while exploring the often hidden elements of how we address our spiritual and personal growth along the journey.

—Will Marre, author of *Save the World and Still Be Home for Dinner*

Greg Voisen's life is a testimony to breakthrough thinking and the entrepreneurial spirit. His new book lays out a fascinating process for moving virtually anything from inspiration to innovation. For me, *Hacking the Gap* is a powerful reminder that dreams without action are just wishes.

—Dan Zadra, best-selling author of *5 (Where will you be 5 years from today?)*

If you want to be the best version of yourself but are confused about how to get there...if you're dreaming of a better life but don't know how to start living your dream...Greg Voisen can help. How? By showing you how to "hack the gap" between where you are today and where you want to be. He can help you cross gaping career chasms and leapfrog limiting beliefs because he's done all that and more in his own remarkable life. This book is his gift to the world; use it wisely and it will be a great gift in your world.

—Phil Bolsta, author of *Through God's Eyes:*
Finding Peace and Purpose in a Troubled World

Innovation is essential to business success. But too many entrepreneurs overlook its most essential starting point: that still, small voice within. As Greg Voisen shows, when you learn to harness your intuition, you'll become a better businessperson—plus, a better person.

—Dorie Clark, author of *Reinventing You* and *Stand Out*,
and adjunct professor, Duke University's Fuqua School of Business

This book is about how to nurture your soul, how to listen intently to the dreams inside you, and embark on a journey to transform those dreams into reality. With deep experience and an uplifting voice, Greg takes you on a journey through his own life experiences while he teaches you how to find your own voice, listen to your intuition, and make courageous decisions. This is an urgent read. After all, how else will you know how to balance your "being" with your "doing?"

—G. Shawn Hunter, author of the bestseller, *Small Acts of Leadership*

A great read from a guy who's wise enough and grounded enough to learn from his own intuition. Greg makes a great case for inner balance and shows why it matters to stay tuned into the inner world.

Hacking the G↔P

a Journey from
INTUITION to INNOVATION and BEYOND

March 2018,
Gina,
You are a most
wonderful, dear
spiritual adventure buddy.
Enjoy Hacking the
Gap.
for now!
Greg

GREG VOISEN

First Edition
Hacking the Gap: A Journey from Intuition to Innovation and Beyond/ Greg Voisen. — first edition.

ISBNs: 978-0-9990-0520-0 (hardcover), 978-0-9990-0522-4 (paperback), 978-0-9990-0521-0 (epub)
1) Personal Growth 2) Business 3) Mastery

Dedication and Acknowledgements

I first want to dedicate this book to my family. My wife Lisa, sons Sean and Chad. My world has been shaped by your love and support for me and I am truly grateful. You have enriched my life immensely.

I need to acknowledge some very special people, coaches and individuals that have been strong influences throughout my life. Grant Bening for being like a second dad after losing my father at a very young age. David Winkelman for always taking my calls and providing great advice and support throughout writing this book. Reese Harris for your dedication, support and loving conversation and heartfelt understanding. Alexa Rosenthal, Ollie Paterson for your tireless support while we discussed my branding, websites and positioning. You are masters and I so appreciate you hanging in through my indecisiveness. Michael Rohde for your wildly creative illustrations, and to Kathy Sparrow and Rick Lineback, my dedicated editors and coaches through this book development project.

To all my friends, clients and associates that have journeyed with me. For picking me up when I was down, and providing kind words I love you all and hope you will enjoy *Hacking the Gap—A Journey from Intuition to Innovation and Beyond.*

To all the great 625+ authors I have interviewed over the 10+ years, you have been my learning ground, my subsistence to forge a new path in life. Your knowledge and wisdom is unsurpassed, you have been my university of personal growth and mastery. I love you all and appreciate you more than you can imagine.

And last but not least to my parents. To my father Eugene H. Voisen who has been long deceased but still lives in my heart, and to my amazing Mother Jean E. Voisen for the most practical advice about how to live life and prosper. I will never forget you. May you both rest in peace. Your son, Greg.

Contents

Foreword

There is a fascinating story of an enlightened king of ancient India who instructed his eager disciple to fill two vessels to the brim with oil. He was to walk through the king's palace, carrying one vessel in each hand, and see each room without spilling a drop of oil. When he returned to the king, he said, "Master, I have done as you have asked and I have not spilled a single drop of oil." The king asked him to describe what he saw. Dismayed, the disciple answered "Sir, I cannot tell you anything about the rooms—I was concentrating on not spilling the oil!" "Go back, then, my son, and go to every room, and when you come back, tell me about each room and also do not spill any oil."

Metaphorically speaking, the universe is beckoning each of us to do the same. There is a gap between our good intentions and our skill and understanding of how to actually manifest those intentions. In *Hacking the Gap*, Greg Voisen shows us how to do it. In personal accounts, in numerous examples, and drawing on his wisdom from life experiences, Greg presents his system of increasing those ah-hah moments and of accessing our voice of intuition, our soul's voice. He leads us through the necessary steps: from insight and capturing these gifts from the universe to igniting and managing our energy, inspiring us to actually implement these ideas into products or services that will have a positive impact on the world.

As I read and absorbed *Hacking the Gap*, I realized that Greg has put together a manual for achieving true success in life. He has outlined the real definition of success, which has more to do with *how* we live and how we get in touch with "being" rather than making "doing" our primary objective. But he does not leave out the practical side. Both are important and achieving a balance between them is the real key. Most of us have concentrated, probably without realizing it, on the doing and the endless reasons and methods we create and believe in our minds to get to the goal. *Hacking the Gap* eloquently reminds us that, contrary to what the monkey mind often tells us, we must try to appreciate each moment, each magical gap in time that invites us to experience the *now* more fully. *Then* we can really carry those vessels of "oil" of all of our many duties in life more effectively and with greater ease and, at the same time, receive those intuitive and unique gifts of "seeing the palace" of creative awareness, which the universe is trying to reveal to us all the time anyway.

If we are really honest with ourselves, we know deep inside us that there's more than just surviving, more than just eating, sleeping, going to work, watching movies, and so forth. We intuitively know that we have infinite potential. And manifesting at least some of that potential is really the only purpose of our being here. Greg Voisen inspires us to *know* that it is possible and he gives us techniques and a methodology to stretch both in our thinking and actions to *hack the gap.*

One of the things I think is important to bring out about *Hacking the Gap* is the experience that Greg draws from in his career and his life. Even though he emphasizes the incomparable benefits of learning to go into the "being" state, which might be as simple as a walk in nature, daily meditation, or just taking a deep breath in the midst of a heavy workload, Greg Voisen is a "doer" from the word go. He has interviewed more than 625 authors as a part of his career and he is a born entrepreneur. He is not a stranger to taking risk, preferably calculated risk, as he explains in his book. This unique combination of being a real go getter and having to learn how to slow down a bit, learn about meditation and the spiritual side of life, qualifies him to speak to a very broad audience. Greg has an easy-going nature about him. His writing voice is conversational and very accessible. As a writer and student of meditation myself, I urge you to take this book, read it from cover to cover, and use it as a ready reference for inspiration, learning to accelerate and increase the number of your insights and ideas, and accessing your own inner genius.

At the end of each chapter, Greg offers step-by-step exercises and suggestions, which he calls Mindset Applications for Hacking the Gap. One of the important themes that appears throughout the book is *resistance*—the kind that gets us stuck in a negative space and can sometimes last for years or a whole lifetime. "Resistance is futile," says the author. "The harder we resist our un-pleasurable life experiences, the slower we will learn from those experiences." This is just one of many jewels of wisdom that Greg Voisen offers in his book.

Because of his background of not only drawing from many sources but also his extensive interviews with writers, Greg is a master of finding the right quote at the right time. Just one example, in the chapter on Ignition—Energy Management he quotes Dr. Jim Loehr and Tony Schwartz in their book, *The Power of Full Engagement: Managing Energy, Not Time is the Key to High Performance and Personal Renewal*. The authors state, "Every one of our thoughts, emotions, and behaviors has an energy consequence for better or worse. The ultimate measure of our lives is not how much time we spend on this planet, but rather how much energy we invest in the time we have—performance, health, and happiness are grounded in the skillful management of energy." Wow! That one really changed the way I look at my own personal energy.

So, finally, I can't say enough good things about *Hacking the Gap*. I feel blessed that I know Greg personally and am privileged to have worked with him on several occasions. This just may well be a new classic in the making. Enjoy, and please use it to turn your creative insights and ideas into something that will change the world!

—**Marshall Goldsmith, author of the #1** *New York Times* **bestseller,** *Triggers*

Introduction

*"You have to leave the city of your comfort and go into the
wilderness of your intuition. What you'll discover will be wonderful.
What you'll discover is yourself."*
—Alan Alda

Throughout my career, I have faced many obstacles and challenges in finding ways to accomplish my goals and manage my responsibilities more effectively—with outcomes that met with my expectations. Often those attempts have resulted in a losing battle. However, I have discovered ways to **Hack the Gap** which by definition is *"The shortest distance between two points, encountering the least amount of resistance, growing personally and professionally, and optimizing your human potential."* Over the years, I've shared my discoveries with hundreds of clients who have engaged me to provide advice and obtain improved results in their businesses, with the added value that they have grown personally and professionally.

Ironically, while giving this advice, I personally became the testing grounds for many of the ideas that I will be sharing with you throughout this book. Many of these ideas worked and produced successful results, while many did not. The lessons I learned from both the successes and failures has strengthened my passion to keep trying to find new ways to work more effectively and to find better ways of **Hacking the Gap** in all areas of my life.

"ALL I NEED TO DO IS LET GO TO REACH THE GOAL. IT COULDN'T BE EASIER!"

Before I go any further, it is important to give you some context on how I acquired my knowledge, expertise, and wisdom, by way of background, education, and business experiences. I will keep this brief, just to give you a perspective of the make-up of my personal character and work ethics.

I am a serial entrepreneur with many start-ups to my credit. I decided to embark on the entrepreneur path very early in life. My first business venture was called Lenny's Bar & Grill, (Lenny is short for Leonard, my birth first name). At eight years of age, I set up a fort behind our family's garage, with a borrowed barbeque, paper plates, plastic utensils, and all the fixings. It was great! I was selling hamburgers, hot dogs, potato salad, and candy to all my friends. I would walk through the neighborhood letting my friends know that Lenny's Bar & Grill was open for business. I even made up a flyer as an invitation to join us at Lenny's Bar & Grill for some fine fixings. In my eyes, this first venture into business was a huge success. I was making a little extra spending money; the only thing I forgot about was the cost of goods. My parents were paying for the hamburgers, hot dogs, candy, and soft drinks that

I was selling. All I had to do was cook the food and collect the money. You can be assured this was not a moneymaking venture for my parents, but I learned a very early lesson in entrepreneurship about how to market and sell. My parents never asked for a return of their invested capital, and I was very appreciative for this interest and debt-free opportunity as a young, eager businessman.

While in high school I opted to open several businesses. My first venture was with a good friend of mine who was Hawaiian, and he convinced me that selling puka necklaces would be a great move. He was my supplier, and I was the distributor/salesman. I sold the puka necklaces to whoever would purchase them—and received lots of orders from the kids at school. I went door-to-door to the local surf shops in town and sold the puka necklaces wholesale to the shop owners. I soon became known as the "Puka King," selling strands of puka beads throughout San Diego County.

The next business venture while still in high school was with my good friend Dwight Johnson. I got the wild idea, while on a trip with him to Santa Fe and Albuquerque, New Mexico, that I would purchase turquoise squash blossom necklaces, along with turquoise rings and bracelets and bring them back to San Diego and sell them to friends and family. Talk about risk! I used all of my savings at the time which was about $1,000 to purchase the jewelry. We transported the jewelry across state lines in the VW Van without incident or duty, by hiding the merchandise under the seats. Upon my return to San Diego, I called on local shops, and vendors as well as friends and family and doubled the money I invested in the jewelry. I made a 100% return on the invested capital, which was a considerable sum of money for a high school kid.

I graduated from high school six months early and decided to take a three-month excursion to Europe upon graduation. While I was there traveling the countryside on my Eurarail Pass, I met a young Swedish man by the name of Sven Benediktusson. After hours of talking and traveling together in Germany, I asked him about unusual items that were unique to Sweden. You guessed it—as we talked I found out that Sweden was known for making really cool clogs, and they were not yet fashionable in the United States. I had another entrepreneurial flash. I could import clogs into the United States from Sweden—thus my career as a "clog" salesman began.

I imported clogs through my new friend and called on local stores in North San Diego County selling clogs to men and women who spent long hours on their feet. I eventually solicited doctors and nurses who worked in the operating rooms of hospitals. It was a great business, but the reliability of receiving the merchandise on a timely basis from Sweden was really a challenge. Also, stocking the inventory to supply males and females with different sizes, colors, and styles was quite an issue. After eighteen months in business, I imported my last shipment of clogs and called it quits.

GREG VOISEN AS A YOUNG MAN EXPLORING THE UNEXPLORED ENTREPRENEUR WITHIN.

My challenges with all of these ventures was that I was only working part-time on the businesses, and once I purchased the goods—be it squash blossoms, puka necklaces or clogs—I did not have the buying capacity to obtain great pricing because my capital investment was not enough to get the deep discounts necessary to have high enough margins to remain in the business. I did have connections in Sweden, Santa Fe, and Hawaii, but my suppliers lost interest after my purchases of merchandise became sporadic and did not meet the volumes they required. These lessons learned in high school were invaluable relative to importing, selling, and managing business finances.

The biggest lesson was that we can either work hard or we can work smart. I wouldn't say that I was particularly working smart, but I was learning from my mistakes and found new ways of taking the easier road to success, thus *Hacking the Gap*. Everything we do in business prepares us for *Hacking the Gap*—to move from our ideas to implementation with much greater ease, grace and speed—and to do so with less resistance both personally and from the outside world.

After tackling the inconsistencies and challenges associated with importing and selling both retail and wholesale merchandise, my next venture was just as a salesman without the risks of sourcing, storing, and financing the purchase of the merchandise.

I decided to take up my hand as a Fuller Brush salesman. While all the other high schools kids were working jobs at Jack in the Box or McDonald's, I decided to sell Fuller Brush products. I know it probably doesn't sound glamorous, but it beat flipping burgers (remember I already had experience flipping burgers at Lenny's Bar & Grill). Fuller Brush provided me with the salesman bag that held all of my essential samples, and I had a route, calling on people

door-to-door. I sold everything from horsehair brushes to air fresh-
eners and household cleaners. I was really well suited for this type
of work and thoroughly enjoyed every minute of the pursuit of
new customers. I had clients who would purchase and repurchase
from me and were very generous with the volume of their orders. I
remember people telling me that they had not seen a Fuller Brush
salesman in years, and their orders reflected that fact. I consistently
earned about $400 per week as a commissioned salesman, and
would frequently receive bonuses on top of that—remember this
was 1972 and part-time after school generating $400 per week was
really great money for a teenage kid.

At this point in my story, you probably have gleaned that the drive
to be an entrepreneur and salesman runs deep, and that I enjoy the
whole process of innovation. You also realize that I am not afraid
of risk and I am willing to do things that are out of the box. My
love of start-up ventures has been a lifetime passion that likely will
not end anytime soon.

I love pursuing new ideas, ventures, and exciting technologies that
will change the world. Often I am the early adaptor, the tester, and
guinea pig for many of the technology products being introduced
into the marketplace today. I really have a passion for exploring,
discovering, and finding new ways of *Hacking the Gap* that make
our work as business owners and entrepreneurs cutting edge, innovative, fulfilling and rewarding.

Life's Twists and Turns

I learned from my father at an early age the meaning of hard work
and taking risks. My father packed up our family and moved to
Southern California in 1963 to help his brother in the construction
business. He was following his dream to join my uncle who was

a building contractor in a small city outside of Los Angeles called Clairemont, California. My father and uncle were probably the biggest risk takers I had ever encountered, except for maybe the guy in the circus who walked the high-wire with no net.

I remember going with my uncle to the savings and loan. I was only nine years old and my uncle left the bank with a check for $1,000,000 to fund the building of his tract homes—and this was in the early 1960s when a $1,000,000 was a significant sum of money. As time went on and my uncle's construction company was flourishing, he needed someone to landscape the model homes. He approached my father, and my dad thought that this would be a good way for him to start up his own business, thus the birth of a landscaping company called *Blue Ribbon Landscape*. My father did all the landscaping for the model homes, and subsequently for the property owners who purchased the homes that my uncle built.

Yet, as for many, life had its ups and downs for both my father and uncle, but one thing for certain was that they both provided a wonderful life for their families. The lessons learned from each of them were innumerable—the biggest and best lesson was *never give up*. When adversity is facing us head on, we find a way to persevere. We apply our talents and skills, and if we don't have the appropriate skills, we learn from others and then apply our newfound skills. My father and uncle were masters at *Hacking the Gap*. They found ways to improve their efficiencies and try new ways of mastering a skill. My personal ability to be persistent when faced with adversity is a direct lesson from my father and my uncle. I'd never encountered two men who worked so hard to make a better life for themselves and for their children and families.

I also witnessed how hard work would take its toll on our family. In 1972, our family moved to San Diego, and in 1975, my father passed away from a massive aneurism and heart attack. This was devastating for our entire family, but the impact on my mother was one of complete heartbreak and emotional breakdown. My mother was in her mid-fifties with no experience running a landscaping company, let alone a business as demanding as the landscaping business was. I had three older brothers, but none of them really wanted to get involved in the business so I stepped up and ran the company with fifteen employees, while taking fifteen credits at San Diego State University to get my Bachelor of Science in Business Management.

Talk about a horrific workload! This demanding pace ultimately caught up with me, and on my nineteenth birthday, I collapsed on our kitchen floor from what I am going to term as a nervous breakdown. I was burning the candle at both ends for too long, and something had to give—and that something was me.

This major turning point prompted great introspection about everything in my life. I questioned my personal beliefs, my work life, and the incredible impact and toll this had taken on both my physical and mental health. I knew that I had to make a change and that I couldn't continue to keep up the pace that was required to run the business and attend school. At this intense pace, I would end up having more physical health challenges. My father's voice echoed in my head—*"Get your education; don't be like me with an eighth grade education."* So I opted to sell the company, give the funds to my mother for her support, and return to San Diego State University full time to complete my degree.

Up to this point in my life, I knew nothing but hard work. That mantra had been programmed into my DNA by both my parents. Don't get me wrong; hard work is not a bad thing, but working smarter is far easier and takes much less of a toll on your life. I believe that learning how to *Hack the Gap* and to innovate a life that is filled with meaning, reward, and success is a much more balanced and worthwhile path to pursue while giving time to enjoy the fruits of your labors.

Listening to Your Soul Calling

As a result of all the pain I had experienced, I had glimpses of a better way. I knew that this would include finding guidance from my inner guidance counselor. I urgently needed to hear the voice from a higher power. So I started on a path in my twenties of reading and listening to the words from Terry Cole Whittaker who was affiliated with the First Church of Religious Science.

Attending her sermons and reading Ernest Holmes books, I was exposed to a very positive way of living my life. This lead to listening to personal growth tapes from Nightingale Conant and Norman Vincent Peale. I can remember driving for hours from one appointment to the next listening to the inspirational messages from hundreds of positive, motivating, and inspiring people.

This positive content opened my mind and my heart. It healed my personal pain and suffering that so desperately needed healing. It allowed me to access my soul for the first time and listen to a small inner voice that wanted me to be healthy, happy, and have a fulfilling life. Over time, this state of consciousness would ebb and flow. I had not become a master at calling in my soul's voice. I didn't always hear the voice of my intuition because it was drowned out by the stronger voice of the ego.

However, as a result of continuing to listen to and reinforce my soul's voice, that calm voice of inner intuition, I discovered a better way, one that allowed me to experience a connection to God. I had my faith reinforced, and my life changed in a way that impacted how I expressed myself to the world. People took notice, and my life became more in sync, and I was having greater insights into who and what I wanted to become and experience in life.

By focusing on and listening to my inner voice, my intuition, my soul—or whatever term you might choose to use—I found my true life work and calling. And so can you. This is not a dream; you can do it just like myself and thousands of others I have encountered on the personal and spiritual growth journey. This is the purpose for me writing this book—to suggest ways that might help you and others on the path of return—the return to your true self.

If my personal story and the stories of others that I will share with you as part of this book move you to take action, then I have accomplished my goal. If you truly listen, and take action on your intuition, then I have inspired you to explore new ways of *Hacking Your Own Gap.*

You will awaken with new ideas, projects, and initiatives—and have the drive and ambition to see them through. My illustrator and I created a visual of what I believe the *Hacking the Gap* process looks like. On the next page is the chart that explains the steps in the process. I hope you relate; but if you don't, don't sweat it—there will be lots of supporting evidence as you continue reading the book.

Remember, all your attempts at inventing something new or making a modification to an existing product or service don't have to be successes; you are going to have failures. The key is to listen to your intuition (your voice), follow the guidance, and take risks. Nothing will happen if you don't take risks.

Thomas Edison said about his thousands of attempts at inventing the light bulb, "I have not failed, I have just found 10,000 ways that won't work."

So let's embark on this journey together exploring how to *Hack the Gap*, and move your inspired ideas and dreams into reality. Let's work on you manifesting those ideas into something tangible, and something that will change the world for the better.

INTUITION
Listening Deeply

CHAPTER 1

Developing the Voice of Intuition

"The intuitive mind is a sacred gift and the rational mind is a faithful servant. We have created a society that honors the servant and has forgotten the gift."
—Albert Einstein

Definition of Intuition: "A natural ability or power that makes it possible to know something without any proof or evidence: a feeling that guides a person to act a certain way without fully understanding why."
—Merriam-Webster's Learner's Dictionary

Where Does Intuition Emanate From?

The voice inside that speaks to us and guides us is something that is developed over years. It requires that we tune in and listen. In our world today, we are distracted by much of the noise from the outside word, and it can be difficult to fine tune to the frequency where intuition resides.

During one point in my career, I co-created a course called "Never Mind the Noise" with my eldest son Sean. At the time the course was in development, my son had been diagnosed with Chronic Mylogonic Leukemia, and our entire family was immersed in exploring the delicate balance between life and death. We were seeking to find the balance in life between the everyday demands and that place of inner calm that brings real meaning to all of life's experiences. What we discovered is that the "noise" from the outside world is so enticing that if you are not incorporating ways to eliminate the noise—through meditation, contemplation, mind- fulness, or any technique that is bringing awareness of the "now"— that this present moment, which is all we ever have in life, will not be fully experienced. And without living in the moment, we cannot hear the voice of wisdom that resides within us. The real purpose of all these techniques it to bring us into this state of awareness. This is when the magic starts to happen!

This elusive voice can be drowned out by the voice of our ego, the one that affirms, "You are not enough." Remember, we usually don't just turn on a switch and hear our inner guidance counselor. As crazy as it may sound, we need to practice getting in touch with our intuition to override the voice of the ego. The ego voice brings fear into our life and persuades us to disbelieve in ourselves.

Tuning into our intuition and really listening and following the guidance takes an act of "knowing" that this small voice is true. It requires trust that our soul's voice is providing guidance and direction in our life that will help us achieve our dreams and not douse them.

Yet, turning away from the noise to listen to the voice of wis- dom, our soul's voice, is not easy. Family members beg for us not to work so hard; employers want us to invest more time, and clients want us to be on call morning, noon, night, and weekends. Because we often fear that we're not good enough, we acquiesce to the demands from the outside world, calling us to do more and be more. It isn't that doing more or being more is a bad attribute or goal to seek—but when it influences us to the point that we cannot hear our true voice and follow our calling, then we are out of balance. We continually engage in negative self-dialogue, that is swirling around in our head, telling us to work harder and do more! It can be immobilizing and create fears and apprehensions that are not true.

However, to end this ceaseless tirade of the ego intimating that we have to do more to make up for our inadequacies, we must learn to be still and listen, and that is hard work regardless of what all the mindfulness and meditation practitioners tell us! Being still and listening has been one of the most difficult states of consciousness for me to reach and sustain, primarily because I know that I have tendencies of attention deficit disorder. I have challenges reaching a meditative state of consciousness because my monkey-mind keeps speaking to me while I am seeking to attain the state of emptiness. While I attempt to meditate daily to assist in attaining an altered *now* state of being, I don't attain this state as often as I would like.

The truth of the matter is that we can always be busy chasing the small and usually unimportant tasks, but it takes courage to listen to our intuition and to follow our dreams. We distract ourselves from the quiet time so we won't have to face becoming all that we can become. It is a way to avoid reaching our greatness, and this is a sad story for most people. We're afraid of becoming all that we are capable of becoming.

Steve Pressfield, the author of *The War of Art*, refers to this as "resistance," saying that,

> **"Resistance presents us with a series of plausible, rational justifications for why we shouldn't do our work."**

When we master the "still" mind state, we are ready and open to hear our intuition. It speaks to us about our dreams and ambitions, and encourages us to go for it. It helps to inspire new ideas, provides us with confidence, and reassures us that we are making the right decisions.

Tony Robbins, in *Awaken the Giant Within*, says,

> "Enjoy making decisions. You must know that in any moment a decision you make can change the course of your life forever: the very next person you stand behind in line or sit next to on an airplane, the very next phone call you make or receive, the very next movie you see or book you read or page you turn could be the one single thing that causes the floodgates to open, and all of the things that you've been waiting for to fall into place. If you really want your life to be passionate, you need to live with this attitude of expectancy."

Mastery of the state of expectancy harkens in a flow of ideas that could be our next big invention or that idea that could change the world. It might seem like a long way from an idea to implementation, and frequently it is, but at least we are on the journey of doing something meaningful. Something that inspires us and gives us a reason to wake up in the morning and put our best efforts into the project we are working to manifest.

Differentiating between Our Ego's Voice & Our Soul's Voice

The voices of the ego and the soul can usually be successfully differentiated by developing a "knowing," a "certainty" about our voice. There are differences between the tone of the voice and the content of the messages. The soul's voice speaks with compassion and understanding, and it is not a condemning or judgmental voice. It is always affirming and nurturing. Our soul's voice speaks in the way we would like to be spoken to by a very understanding, compassionate friend or coach. When we hear it, we have a sense of peace, we are feeling hopeful, and we find an alternative path that leads us to a new horizon. Our spirit is lifted, and we have a true understanding about what really "is." We are open to new ideas and suggestions. Our resistance is removed, and we are a vessel for all like-minded souls to help us on our path of return.

On the flip side of the coin, the voice of the ego is judgmental, condemning, and reinforces what we are "not." It attempts to instill fear, disbelief, and misunderstanding about how and what we really can become. When the voice of the ego speaks, we can feel belittled and depressed. We can feel trapped and directionless. If freedom is what the soul provides in its conversations with us, then the ego instills a feeling of imprisonment, and we struggle with not knowing the best path toward fulfillment and joy. If we allow the ego to take over our consciousness, we will become paralyzed to take action.

your TRUE VOICE

"MY TRUE VOICE IS ALWAYS WITH ME. ALL I NEED IS TO STOP, BREATHE AND LISTEN."

Wayne Dyer once said this about the ego:

> "The ego is only an illusion, but a very influential one. Letting the ego-illusion become your identity can prevent you from knowing your true self. Ego, the false idea of believing that you are what you have or what you do, is a backwards way of assessing and living life."

The ego voice is not all bad. It is here to protect us and we will never eliminate the ego voice. In fact, we have no need to eliminate it. Its job is to take direction from the soul's voice—to get the job done after we've been inspired by our intuition. We need to learn how to control our ego voice. This is accomplished by first understanding how to recognize the difference between the ego and soul voices. And this takes practice, awareness, and attentiveness to the voices within us. It requires that we **"Never Mind the Noise."**

To accomplish the feat of differentiating these two voices, we must give praise to the voice from our soul, and speak in a firm and commanding way to our voice of ego. It's necessary to put the ego voice in its place as if it was a child in need of good boundaries. And you are the one who sets those boundaries. Your soul's voice, on the other hand, knows no boundaries. It is a free spirit, like you are becoming as you evolve your consciousness.

Mark Nepo, author of *The One Life We're Given*, says,

> "In the relationship between our soul and our will [ego], our soul is like a sail. Once hoisted in the open, our soul is filled by the wind of Spirit, and that wind establishes our course and direction. Our will is its rudder. Its job is to follow where the soul filled with Spirit leads us. Our soul shows us where to go, while our will helps to steer our way there."

Determining the Validity of Your Intuition

Our intuition is not a separate something that is not part of who we are. It is not a feeling that is outside of us knocking to get it. It is always within us, just waiting for us to listen and hear what it has to say. It wants to guide us and give proper direction. I would caution that one must be discerning about the voice of intuition. It takes practice and time to discern truth from fiction. This feeling arises in me as being clairsentience (an extremely heightened form of empathy or "clear feeling"). Others may experience voices which means they are clairaudient. No matter how we experience our intuitions, it requires both sides of our brain to make the ultimate decision on whether or not to act on our intuitions.

Judith Orloff, PhD, a Los Angeles–based intuitive psychiatrist and author of *Second Sight* believes the benefits of listening to your instincts go far beyond making good on life-or-death decisions. "Living more intuitively demands that you're in the moment," she says, "and that makes for a more passionate life."

But she also notes that gut instincts are far from infallible. The right brain's skill with pattern identification can trigger suspicions of unfamiliar (but not dangerous) things, or cause you to be especially reactive to people who simply remind you of someone else.

So how do you choose which gut feelings to trust? Orloff suggests that it's a matter of "combining the linear mind and intuition," and striking the right balance between gut instinct and rational thinking. Once you've noticed an intuitive hit, she says, you can engage your rational mind to weigh your choices and decide how best to act on them.

As we move through this fast-paced world, it is easy to get distracted and lose focus, as our attention is being drawn in multiple directions. Almost all of us deal with interruptions in the form of emails, phone calls, meetings and other distractions that can consume not only our valuable time, but also overload our ability to accomplish that which deserves our greatest attention. We jump from one project to another at a pace that almost never provides time to listen to that inner voice of intuition that so wants to speak to us. That voice encourages us when we are down, or uplifts us to keep moving forward in spite of the adversity. It could even provide valuable insight that might change the course of a project or even our lives.

Listening to the voice of intuition is like tuning your radio to the correct channel—the intuitive channel. Sometimes we get two channels competing for the airwaves. Once we are tuned into the *intuitive channel*, we will hear that voice speaking to us or feel through our senses what needs to be accomplished. We will be guided in the right direction. The most important thing is to tune in, listen, and follow the advice as long as we have checked in with the logical mind to affirm we are on the right path. We will awaken to a new way of seeing and being in the world. We realize that much of what we perceive to be true really is not true at all. We go around making up stories that are not true about ourselves, then spend a tremendous amount of time convincing ourselves that these stories were not true so we can make our life better. Insidious behavior takes us in circles, usually with no way out until we become aware that this is the behavior that causes insanity. Banish the ideas and thoughts that state, "I'll never get this right," or "I will never have enough time," or "I am not enough." Those thoughts are rubbish. We are enough and our soul wants us to express who and what we have come here to become.

Determining the validity of our intuition takes time and patience. We will know when we have tuned into the correct channel because the voice that we hear or the feeling we experience will resonate in our heart and soul. It will feel comfortable and affirming. It will encourage you to make giant moves forward and get out of the inertia of life. It will praise you for your courage and persistency in life.

So give yourself permission to step away from the noise of emails, text messages, and phone calls. Give yourself permission to listen to the stillness and wisdom inside of you.

Defining and Closing the Gap

When we are *Hacking the Gap*, we are able to move more definitely toward our life's goals and dreams. "Hacking" is about finding ways to achieve our ultimate dreams and goals in a shorter period of time, with less resistance, while in the process have the life experiences and personal growth required to make the journey meaningful—and enjoyable. It is about reaching our desired human potential and continuing the act of practicing what makes the journey easier—which means quieting those mental thoughts and beliefs that are keeping us from reaching our full human potential. We can reframe our mindset through affirmations, mantras, meditation, reading, journaling and practicing staying present and in the "now."

And how do you know if you're on the right track? Look for clues along the way. Synchronicity will appear. You'll be in the flow. Phone calls from someone you may be thinking of, hearing a meaningful song on the radio, or seeing a sign that recalls a memory of someone or something.

"WHEN I STAY IN *flow* I AM OPEN TO MORE IDEAS, AND GREATER FREEDOM."

Charlene Belitz and Meg Lundstrom write in *The Power of Flow,*

> "Flow is at work when things fall into place, obstacles melt away, our timing is perfect, and whatever is necessary—money, work, people, opportunities—appears as needed. Synchronicity is the means by which our way is eased."

So observe the world around you, and look for signs and signals that are speaking to you. It could be as simple as finding a penny on the sidewalk or some symbolism that you recognize in a signpost.

My mother died almost two years ago, and she still sends me pennies from heaven. She is telling me that I am worthy. For years I have been receiving signs from clocks. Invariably, I will look at the clock on the computer, or my watch, or the clock in the car and the time will be 11:11 or 1:11.

What does all this mean? According to numerology, the number 11 possesses the qualities of patience, honesty, spirituality, sensitivity, and intuition and is idealistic and compassionate. Those people who are drawn to 11 operate on a different level of energy than most, and when two people come together who both have this type of energy, it's almost combustible.

11:11 is the universe's way of urging us to pay attention to our heart, our soul and our inner intuition. It serves as a wake-up call to us so that opportunities are not missed in this lifetime. Seeing this particular sequence means that the universe is trying to have us open our eyes and begin paying more attention to the synchronicities around us.

The key for me is to link the signs to something meaningful in my life, something that I might want to take action on or need to pay attention to.

Mindset Applications for Hacking the Gap to Developing the Voice of Intuition

- Spend more time in contemplation and silence. This could be mindfulness practices or meditation both in the morning and evening.

- When working on your computer make sure that you give yourself breaks of about fifteen minutes every hour. You might be saying "really!" Yes, really. You need to get away from the screen to reset your mind and treat yourself to a break.

- Take more time to be in nature. Taking walks on the beach or in the woods is great. But if this is not possible just head to a park or somewhere you can commune with nature. Richard Louv, author of *The Nature Principle*, says, "Reconnecting to the natural world is fundamental to human health, well-being, spirit, and survival."

- Write in your journal for fifteen minutes, three times per week or when you are called to make an entry about something that is meaningful, or an observation you had. Keep it handy or use a digital version such as Penzu (penzu.com).

- Exercise, take yoga classes, tai chi, or anything that gets your body moving. I encourage regular exercise for 60–90 minutes at least three times per week. No matter what you do, just get your body moving. Amazing things happen, including the release of wonderful chemicals into your bloodstream that move you into an altered state of consciousness.

- Pamper yourself. Get a massage, a pedicure, take a sauna. Treat yourself with the ultimate amount of respect and self-care.

- Spend time with friends and family. Community is important. And if you want inspiration and support for your business, join a mastermind group where you can be supported. However, be cautious about the amount of time you spend with others, and make sure the values of those in the groups you spend time with are aligned with your own. American Entrepreneur and motivational speaker, Jim Rohn, said, "We are the average of the five people we spend the most time with." Choose wisely.

- Find a charitable cause to support that is aligned with your values and donate time and money to the cause. There is nothing better than giving back to the community you live in or to a cause that has an effect worldwide. No matter what you do get involved in some way.

- If you don't have a hobby, find one. Play a musical instrument, sing, knit, do crossword puzzles, read, write...anything that activates your mind and keeps you focused—that isn't work related.

- Practice gratitude. Daily write at least three things for which you are grateful for...your health, your family, your opportunities, etc.

The above is just a partial list of actions and practices you can incorporate into your life. Every one of these practices has a natural way of helping you awaken the intuitive voice that is just waiting to speak with you. It will provide you with clues, ideas, and inspiration to move to the next step of manifesting something wonderful in your life. It is the starting point that sparks the ideas which is the next step in the cycle that will move you to manifesting and embracing a change in your life.

And remember,

> **The greatest gift that you can give yourself is a little bit of your own attention.**
> **—author Anthony J. D'Angelo**

What else might you do to *Hack the Gap* and come to know your intuition? What are some activities that you enjoy doing but have put on the back burner because you haven't got the time?

INSIGHT
The Aha Moment

CHAPTER 2

Insight & Aha Moments

"I think the success around any product is really about subtle insights.
You need a great product and a bigger vision to execute against,
but it's really those small things that make the big difference."
—Chad Hurley, co-founder and former CEO of YouTube.com

Pinballs of Connectivity

How many of you reading this book remember the pinball machine? If you do, then great! If you don't, pinball machines were the predecessor to the digital games that we currently have on our smartphones and computers.

Imagine if you were feeling the metal flippers beneath your fingers, hearing the bells and dings as the metal balls pings off one of the posts in the pinball machine. See the flashing lights as you score more points and move up levels of proficiency. The idea of the game is to score as many points as possible to either beat your personal best, or the best of another player and win the bragging rights of being the *champion*!

"I CAN CONNECT THE DOTS OF CONNECTIVITY TO REACH
THE HIGHEST PINNACLE OF CREATIVITY *and* INNOVATION."

Pinball machines take me back to a time when I was quite
young—a time when my father was repairing pinball machines
and jukeboxes in bars and drive-in diners. I would accompany him
on his routes. I remember he carried a gun in his holster to protect
himself, he was assigned the job of emptying the machines of all
the money—mostly quarters, dimes, and nickels. I would help him
carry the bags of money back to the car. I have fond memories of
accompanying my father on his routes, playing skeet ball, pinball,
and listening to the jukeboxes and collecting money from the various gaming machines.

The lessons learned by watching people get memorized by the
pinball machines were indelible. They were fixed to these machines
much like the people who play slot machines in Las Vegas.

I always wondered how someone could get so affixed to wanting to compete with himself or herself to beat previous scores, to set a new record in an attempt to earn more money and bragging rights. I found my answer in a May 2013 article in *Runner's World* by Michelle Hamilton:

> Mentally tough athletes are positive thinkers and process-oriented. *"If you focus on results, you take yourself out of the now,"* says Stan Beecham, Ph.D., sports psychologist for two elite running groups, McMillan Elite and Zap Fitness. *"And it's the now that allows for the results later."* He compares it to football: *In the pregame huddle, a good coach won't tell his team to go out and win, he'll say, go out and pass well, tackle hard. Those are the steps that lead to scoring and winning. If runners do the same, the results will come.*

My point of using the analogy of the pinball machine and desire to beat our best is that it is all about focusing on connecting the balls with the pegs as often as possible so that we reach a new best. Throughout life, we are attempting to connect the dots so we can perform at our best.

This analogy is similar to us making connections in our mind by drawing on the subconscious reserve that has been collecting experiences, learning, and information since we were born. All the information stored in our subconscious mind is a goldmine. The key is recalling this information, (the learnings, information, and senses that are being stimulated) and connecting it to the new data that is being collected through our observation and awareness.

When we are able to accomplish this successfully we have an *aha moment*—an insight about something. It might be about something we have been contemplating, or having fleeting thoughts about, but when it all connects—*Eureka*! These strokes of genius have birthed the development of a new product or service, and can encourage us to take action with the results being that our personal lives transform forever.

"I THINK I'VE GOT A
GREAT NEW PRODUCT IDEA!"

The Realization of Convergence & Awareness

Convergence is the connecting of the dots between our subconscious and the immediate live feed of data from our world in real time. Information, ideas, and thoughts are happening in real time. We are processing about 70,000 thoughts per day according to the National Science Foundation. When we are able to connect these thoughts in real time frequently insightful and aha moments occur. The brain becomes activated, and we connect the synapses in our brain. The result of a moment of connection like this can change our life provided we have the confidence to act on the insight.

These moments of connection don't happen frequently enough for many of us, but as we become more proficient at *Hacking the Gap*, we will find that insightful moments occur more often and our willingness to act on them is more instantaneous. We don't waste time thinking about all the pluses and minuses; we just start to put the process of manifestation in play. We write our plan, call others for advice, and most importantly keep a positive mental attitude about the new insight(s). The act of staying positive is so important to seeing it through to implementation. Remember, it can be a long road from an idea to implementation, but the road is filled with wonder and fulfillment.

Immediately following an aha moment, we internally process the experience and often don't always know what to do about it. It can require a bit of processing both from our gut reaction, and then we usually seek confirmation from others that it is a good idea.

These aha moments have taken my breath away—a sign of surprise and amazement that I connected the dots to arrive at a moment of insight. I feel as if this is a gift from the divine. Listening to my intuition and soul's calling provided the fertile ground of receptivity to manifest something, and usually at the right time in my life when all the stars are aligned.

I believe that the synchronicities that allowed for an experience like this to occur are not just for this one particular event to occur. Something outside of our power is at work guiding and filling in the gaps. It happens because we are aware, open, receptive and willing to listen to the soul voice.

I encourage you *not* to ignore these special moments, for this is a gift and you certainly want to open the gift and find out what's inside. I must state, however, that opening the gift doesn't guarantee instant success. Choosing to move forward with the contents can be a long and daunting journey. If you ask any inventor, he or she will tell you that the pathway they take to manifesting a successful product or service requires tremendous hard work and persistence. Dean Kamen, the inventor of the Segway, refers to this invention as a ten-year overnight success. Manifesting our ideas takes patience and action.

Awareness and presence with this moment of inspiration are just the first step on this path to innovation, but it can be the most exciting. Learn to savor these moments, for if you choose to manifest this idea into reality, the work is just now beginning—and it is worth every ounce of effort you invest.

Duplicating the Insight and Aha Moments

If you are still reading this book and have come to this juncture, then you realize that I am here to help and guide you to have more of these insightful, aha moments. I want you to access the creative genius the lies within. You will be someone who sees the world differently who is looking for and seeking to duplicate these moments as often as possible. As a creative person, you are unique and you don't fit in the box that the "normal world" would like for you to fit into. You're part rebel, part iconoclast. In other words, you are a thought leader in the world.

Apple co-founder Steve Jobs said,

> "Here's to the crazy ones, the misfits, the rebels, the troublemakers, the round pegs in the square holes....
> the ones who see things differently—they're not fond of rules... You can quote them, disagree with them, glorify

or vilify them, but the only thing you can't do is ignore them because they change things... they push the human race forward, and while some may see them as the crazy ones, we see genius, because the ones who are crazy enough to think that they can change the world, are the ones who do."

And I know we can change the world when we consistently learn the techniques that will assist you in having more of these insightful moments. As you continue to learn and grow, you will be *Hacking the Gap*. You will shorten the time it takes to have more insights. You will be inspired and be willing to take risks. You will be fearless to pursue your dreams, and you will encourage others to take the ride with you. You will attract people who will help propel your dreams. You are not meant to go this alone. Having big ideas and going for it requires that you inspire others to help you manifest the dream. Your ideas will turn into that innovative product, service, or social cause that has lasting and sustainable impacts on the world.

Dream Big, Live Life to its Fullest, and Enjoy Your Journey

Duplicating these aha moments does not have to be hard; with practice, it can become as natural as working on a computer. It does however require preparation and practice. Sustaining our creative energy requires a good balance between being and doing. In the alternating states of being and doing consciousness, we are working to achieve our vision. While in the doing state of consciousness, the synapses are firing and our brain is working overtime just to keep up with the flow of connectivity. We are putting the puzzle together at a rapid pace, and this requires diligence, fortitude, and masterful focus. While in the being state of consciousness, we can relax and allow our mind to be in a free form state. Here the synapses are firing randomly and will then connect to the logical linear left side of our brain. Our creative energies are in overload allowing for more new insights to happen, making it possible to continually improve the original thought or idea.

The process of duplicating our insights requires positive self-talk. Affirmations and mantras, what we read, write and listen to daily, can greatly influence our energy and creative mindset. We need to consistently reinforce our mind with good thoughts and encouraging words.

What affirmations are you saying to yourself to inspire your creative being?

With what kind of self-talk are you reinforcing your subconscious mind? Are they positive or negative?

Most individuals choose one of two paths in life. Those on the learning line are committed to personal and professional growth. They know that the *journey* is an important factor. Those on the goal line are *only* concerned with achieving the goal. Those of us in the process of *Hacking the Gap* are on the learning line, and we're focused on more than a goal. We value how we influence others and can possibly change the world. If you are a continual learner and have an insatiable appetite to learn from others, then you are open to personal growth and change.

Read books, listen to podcasts, and keep a journal. Write about your feelings, ideas, and insights. Record the experience, then read what you have written. Review them monthly just so you can reaffirm the progress you are making.

Experiencing a greater frequency of insights and aha moments can be hacked. We can "do" this more often, with practice.

As my good friend Stephen Kotler, the co-author of *Abundance: The Future is Better Than You Think,* says:

> "You can hack the state of 'flow'—that place where life unfolds effortlessly. Hacking Flow is about setting up your mind and body for optimal breakthroughs and when you do, you'll experience phenomenal results. When your sense of self goes away and your inner critic turns off in Flow, you're no longer judging your ideas so harshly, so again, creativity goes up."

I encourage you to listen to the podcast that I conducted with Steven Kotler that can be heard at www.hackingthegapbook.com

Hacking the Gap is about reaching a state of awareness where we can compress the time between the insightful experiences. It is about shifting our state of consciousness by using proven techniques and technologies that will shift our brain's ability to make connections more rapidly. The synapses will rewire and re-fire in sequences that will create new insights.

Mindset Applications for Hacking the Gap of Insight & Aha Moments

- Create affirmations that are positive and have a future vision. Write the affirmation and post them where you can read them often. I recommend that you reinforce the affirmation daily if possible by citing them aloud. Here's an example: *I am enjoying spreading the message of Hacking the Gap around the world.*

- Read books on topics that you believe will help you foster new ideas and insight moments. There are millions of books published worldwide and found on Amazon, Barnes and Noble, Indi Books, and more—either paper or digital. Order or download something that is out of your wheelhouse, outside your norm, and see how you feel reading it. Stretching the base of your beliefs and ideas is a good thing. (See a recommended list at the back of this book.)

- Listen to podcasts on a regular basis. Podcasts that assist you in expanding your mind and getting you thinking in a new way. I created a program called *Inside Personal Growth* and have been interviewing authors on topics of personal growth, wellness, business, mastery, and spirituality for over ten years. Go to www.insidepersonalgrowth.com to listen to some of the over 600+ podcasts.

- Imagine if a video camera was following you for the day. Capture your observations of your actions in your journal and review what you wrote. Ask yourself if you like what you did during the day. What might you change or alter to make your day more enjoyable? Did you meet and interact with the people you wanted to?

- Certainly attempt to find reflection time or meditation time in your day, preferably morning and evening.

- Turn off the television or electronic devices at least one-hour prior to retiring to bed for a restful evening.

- Keep a note pad by your bedside. Insights and ideas that manifest don't have a time clock, and I know you will be awakened with ideas you will want to capture. Please capture them no matter how crazy they might seem. Trust your "Crazy Ideas." They often disappear if we go back to sleep without writing them down.

- Relax and unwind. It's not a privilege; it's a necessity to stay balanced, stress-free, and open to new insights. This could be an evening walk, a yoga class or anything that you enjoy doing that alters your mind into a relaxed state of consciousness.

- Remember to plan your day with periodic breaks. As author Terry Hershey says, there is power in the pause. Schedule space between your meetings to regroup and prepare for the next item on your calendar. Provide yourself with time to reflect on previous meetings, maybe even writing up notes on your thoughts.

If you institute these recommended "doings" in your day, then this will assist you in *Hacking the Gap* toward having more insights and aha moments—and ultimately strengthen your ability to "be." Please be patient with yourself. This process is learned, and like any learning, it takes practice and the commitment to making it happen.

Continually reinforce your mind with positive self-talk, and then *perform* actions that are in alignment with the positive self-talk. This practice will lead to the pinballs of connectivity, and your "pinball score" will elevate beyond your expectations.

IDEAS
Capture & Record

CHAPTER 3

IDEAS:
Capturing and Recording Your Brilliance

"Life is like a camera, focus on what is important, capture the good times, develop from the negatives and if things don't work out take another shot."
—Unknown

In the previous chapter, I discussed how to increase the frequency of your insights and aha moments. The best way to improve the frequency and quality of your insights is to place yourself in the environments that stimulate greater frequency. Increase the frequency of your meditations. Take more walks in the park or by the beach. Get out in nature, and commune. Give yourself free time to think, write, and reflect by journaling and or listening to your favorite music.

No matter what the environment, we can set up the conditions so that aha moments increase and are significantly more meaningful. When they do arise, you will need a reliable system to record your ideas. Insights become fleeting thoughts if we don't acknowledge them and capture the insights. Writing them down is the best way to capture any new idea. Creative people keep a notebook of their ideas. The key is to have a system that is simple and very accessible. If you don't have a system to record your insights, ideas and aha moments, they quickly disappear back into the ether. Grab a tape recorder, pen and paper, whiteboard—whatever you feel most comfortable using.

"I'M ALWAYS PREPARED TO CAPTURE MY GREAT IDEAS, AND RECORD THEM."

We never know when something will spark a new idea or trigger the synapsis in our brain and if not captured poof, it's gone—especially those ideas that wake us in the middle of the night. If we are too tired and uninspired to get up and find the paper and pen or pencil to capture the idea, we lose what could be a great idea. I know that my ideas will often come at night, right out of a sound sleep. I usually get up and go to my office, which is downstairs, to write the ideas or words that are coming up for me. I do this for two reasons, one I don't want to turn on the light and wake up my wife, and the second one is that when I get out of bed it usually stimulates more thoughts and the ideas get time to maturate. I frequently will stay up for an hour or longer recording and contemplating my newly developed ideas.

Insights evolve over time and are generally something that we edit and or purge. If we log our ideas in a notebook or journal, purging the list from time to time becomes necessary. Take the time to review your journal or notebook monthly. Reflect and write additional thoughts next to your insights and ideas. This review process is how you take ideas and turn them into *great ideas*. Old ideas evolve into a new product or service that has greater potential than your original idea.

Good ideas, insights, or intuitions emanate from the weaving of your subconscious thoughts along with a realization from the present moment. The weaving of the stored information in your subconscious along with realizations and insights from the present moment are what allow you to connect the dots.

The dictionary defines:

> **"Insight" as "the capacity to gain an accurate and deep intuitive understanding of a person or thing." (unknown)**

This is a wonderful definition because it helps us to understand that insights feed our intuition and vice versa, our intuition inspires new insights.

If you look at the *Hacking the Gap* model below, you will see that the arrows are bi-directional on all of the eight (8) "I's." The reason for this is that all of the steps in the *Hacking the Gap* process are connected, and while they stand alone, they are best developed when we understand the interconnectedness of the steps leading to the manifestation of our ideas. The implementation step can and often times is the most difficult and challenging, but when you are aware of what lies ahead by using the chart as a guide it is easier to navigate the steps. It should also be noted that you might enter into the process at a different stage. You don't always have to enter the creative and innovate process with a spark of intuition. Usually new ideas go through a series of steps before they are developed.

The frequency of our ideas are directly proportional to our ability to tap into our intuition, then transition to the insight stage where you record, capture, and solidify the brilliance of your idea. I once heard that visionaries of organizations come up with

10–20 new ideas every day. They are idea machines—if you are an idea machine, then the journey around the *Hacking the Gap* process from intuition to innovation is easy, but if you are not that fortunate, then segueing from stage to stage can seem like lots of hard work.

I've been blessed with the idea gene; ideas are constantly being sparked and connected in the synapses of my brain. I see a problem, and immediately I am thinking about how I can create a perfect solution. In client meetings, I will be pinging ideas at a very rapid rate. Most clients will say to me that they are unable to keep up with the speed of the ideas that I am developing during our session. I'm fortunate to be put into circumstances where clients are paying me to help solve problems and come up with solutions, and I welcome the challenges.

My consciousness is open to many ideas that instead of turning off the flow, I record all the valuable ideas. I recommend you do the same. Keep an idea journal next to your desk, bedside and in your car. Every time you are inspired, please record and capture the ideas. When your makeup is that of an idea generator, you need a parking lot to hold those ideas—you never know they might come in handy one day. This process frees up the mind space so that the ideas just keep flowing, and it's perfectly fine to postpone action on any of these ideas until it's the appropriate time to evolve the idea into the perfect product or service.

Knowing, Listening, and Ruminating on an Idea

The process of rating your ideas on a scale from "1 to 10" with "10" being the best and "1" being the least valuable idea, allows you to put them in a priority of importance and better understand which ideas might be worth pursuing. When you have created your ordered list of ideas, I recommend that you "check in" with your soul through a process of meditation, and then listen to what the inner voice is telling you about the validity, your knowing, and certainty of this idea. If you have the slightest doubt, then postpone the idea's development until you have an opportunity to validate your idea through research and testing.

Testing your ideas with friends, family, associates, and bouncing the idea off of others can give you "real world" validation. I caution you: *please don't let other people's opinion dampen your ideas or dreams with negativity.* I know you have all heard the stories of people having great ideas, then they listen to someone who doubts the value of the idea, and they don't proceed with the evolution or development of their great idea. Shortly after the idea having being dampened by someone, they read a story or hear something on radio or TV, that their great idea was developed into a new product or service by someone else, and they made millions of dollars, or helped thousands of people. You don't have to be that statistic. You can be the one that follows through and takes the required actions to manifesting your idea into reality.

Insights and aha moments turn often into ideas that inspire us to take action. Ideas are a well-documented account of insights. Through a process of weaving our insights into a well-documented idea we are able to articulate that idea to another interested person with clarity, conviction, and passion. Being able to do this creates awareness and reaffirms that we are on to something big. It takes time and research for us to feel 100% confident to allow our ideas to be exposed to the world. It's important to be careful not to break the news too soon, or on the flip side, hold onto ideas until it is too late, and we are less enthusiastic about our idea. Other people's comments either negative or positive are the fuel that propels us to keep moving forward. And as you build momentum, you are proving to the world that your idea is a good one and something that you trust in enough to invest your time, money and energy to birth it into manifestation.

Again, some of the greatest ideas have gone undeveloped because someone's spirit and ambition was dampened by the negative thoughts and opinions of others. Keeping a positive spirit and mental attitude about what you are doing is imperative. The way you do this is to keep yourself surrounded by positive and uplifting friends and associates.

Steve Maraboli, author of *Life, the Truth, and Being Free*, says,

> **"People who lack the clarity, courage, or determination to follow their own dreams will often find ways to discourage yours. Live your truth and don't EVER stop!"**

This journey of birthing your ideas through the *Hacking the Gap* process and bringing it to market is 50% fortitude and positive mindset. Your positive mindset and your willingness to carry through with the idea—in spite of pessimistic viewpoints from others is what will set you apart from the masses.

Getting Unstuck!

If you are a person who feels like you have not had many great ideas in your life, there is hope. We can all experience long periods of creative blocks. It is if we have lost all touch with our intuition. When creative ideas are not flowing, we become desperate. We often give up on even thinking about breaking the long protracted cycle of being devoid of a great idea.

"I WONDER IF I'LL EVER GET THIS FINISHED?!!"

There are several work arounds that can stimulate and open up your mental and spiritual consciousness to receiving new ideas. The first is to constantly surround yourself with people that are positive and stimulate your thinking. Secondly, start or join a mastermind group of like-minded people. Tell them about your dreams and aspirations, be vulnerable, and see what evolves. Third, would be to read books and articles that are not related to your field of expertise. It has been proven that when you read material that is outside your usual interests, your mind connects the dots more rapidly because you are having your brain fire the synapses in areas of the brain that previously were not activated. To stay in creative flow, this is one of the ways of *Hacking the Gap*.

If you are unable to think of any good ideas of your own, then engage in conversations with your friends and listen to their ideas and become stimulated by the dialogue and conversation. Allow your consciousness to open up to the possibilities.

I recently had an experience of this happening to me. I went to a luncheon meeting with an attorney who I had met, and didn't have any expectation of what the outcome of the meeting would bring.

I was open and stayed engaged by asking questions about him and his practice. During our conversation he revealed to me that he was not practicing law any longer. His practice had evolved into one of mediation with couples going through divorce. What I learned about mediation stimulated my thoughts about how I might use some similar techniques to his with my clients who were dealing with disputes over agreements in business.

Then, as I mentioned to him that I unofficially conducted lots of mediations while working with my clients, an aha moment struck! I could market myself as a mediator without being licensed. This is just one small example, but when we are open and listen we are bound to observe or hear something that will lead to a series of thoughts that will ultimately evolve into another good idea that could very well be implemented into our business or personal life.

Trust that all conversations are divinely created. You are being sourced to receive or send a message that needs to be heard at a specific time to a specific group of people. *Remember the analogy about the pinballs of connectivity?* Conversations, ideas, and insights are all part of the overall master plan, and our role in this master plan is to develop our ideas into something valuable—and that *will make* a positive contribution to the world. A great idea may be about a business, service, book, course, play, or music score. Whatever it may be, we are consciously becoming channels and allowing ourselves to be instruments in this amazing process to create, heal, and embrace others with our creative ideas.

However, deeply tapping into our consciousness by opening up to what our intuition is informing us to do, and listening to the advice and trusting the advice is not as easy as it may seem. I speak from personal experience because there have been many times in my life when I have been challenged by emanating new ideas, and I was just downright "stuck."

Being stuck feels like we are disconnected from our "inner" voice. All we hear is the chatter from the outside world. It is confusing, irritating and stressful. I went through a long stretch of being stuck, and I attribute it to not taking the time to take care of myself, physically, mentally, emotionally, and spiritually. I was a wreck, filled with anxiety and despair about where I was going and where I fit in to what seemed like a confusing and fast paced world.

I had anxiety attacks every day for years. It was debilitating to make moves outside of my safe zone, which was my home and office. I feared at any moment I was going to have another panic attack, and believe me *they are real*—with extreme physical effects.

I would get chest pain, sweat, and hyperventilate to a point where I was light headed feeling like I was going to pass out. When we are dealing with these circumstances in our life, believe me it is tough to even think about being creative. We are not only stuck, we are frozen and the *culprit is fear*!

I was so stressed out that I ultimately went to a cardiologist who did an angiogram and I was told that everything was OK. But I wasn't. I had literally convinced myself to be afraid of the outside world and I was in constant fear. I am pleased to report that I entered a program of biofeedback where I learned how to breathe correctly—imagine that! This awareness evolved into my practice of meditation and mindfulness, and it has now been over twenty years, and I still practice the techniques taught through the biofeedback and have added a very strong practice of meditation.

I have a deep understanding and knowing that when we are chasing the shiny and tantalizing distractions of the world—when we are more caught up into the "what" than the "why," we are going to be hard pressed to *Hack the Gap* into a more natural flow of ideas, ease, and grace of life.

I am convinced that the biggest killer of tapping our intuition, which is the gateway to new ideas, is stress. We live in a society where stress and stress-related illness is prevalent. One of those illnesses is allowing our brains to go into automatic pilot mode, just living our lives without thought, planning, or contemplation.

The best way to get "unstuck" and open up the pathways to our intuition is to remove the "fear" that is causing the stress. Faced with an onslaught of things to do or difficult obstacles, our minds go into the mode of "not being enough" or "not having enough." This is a killer to "intuitive access."

It's difficult, if not impossible at times, to hear our soul's calling when we are in fear. This only creates the atmosphere where doubt and worry arise. This is the opposite of love which is the voice of your soul, where inspiration and hopefulness reside. Learn to love yourself and others around you, and the voice of intuition will not only be heard but you will be able to trust in what you are being told and will learn how to act upon that intuition.

The lessons learned from our "negative" experiences are what stimulate us to access the new ideas, tap into the creative process, and then develop something that will solve not only our problems, but the problems faced by many others faced with the same or similar challenges.

> "Life is simple. Everything happens for you, not to you. Everything happens at exactly the right moment, neither too soon nor too late. You don't have to like it...it's just easier if you do,"

says **Byron Katie**, author of *Loving What Is: Four Questions that Can Change Your Life*.

Remember, tuning into our intuition requires being open and receptive by surrounding yourself with good people and great relaxing and stimulating environments.

We must de-stress. We can't just expect our intuition to tune in through an act of will. We need to dial into the frequency which requires that we tune out the "noise" that is affecting our ability to hear the messages that are just waiting for us to hear.

Jill Willard, the author of *Intuitive Being*, writes:

> "Depending on how we look at the world, we may believe that intuition comes from an outside source that is larger than us—that it is sort of universal knowing or guidance system. Or we may believe that it comes from within us, from a quiet, center space that remains strong, stable, and untouched even in the midst of the chaos of our daily lives. It can be both of these things. Another way to look at intuition is as the integration of what is within us and what is outside of us—that we are all connected in one and the same energy, a form of being within and without at once."

Capturing Your Ideas (Analog & Digital)

We all have tools that we utilize in our work-a-day world to help us capture notes and record events and meetings that are important to us. Those tools can be as simple as a piece of paper and a pencil or as elaborate as mind mapping software. No matter what the tool you utilize to capture your ideas, my recommendation is to err on the side of comfort and ease of use. Your preferences matter.

Whatever medium you use to capture your ideas, be it mp3 recordings, mind mapping software, Evernote, etc., I have some simple tips to integrate them with your particular style and process of working.

First, always have something analog, such as a notebook and a pencil. The reason behind this advice is that you never know when the idea will pop up, and we can't always depend on the fact that your iPad or smart phone will be nearby—or charged—especially in the middle of the night.

However, if you are rarely without your mobile devices, download one of the many simple recording applications for both Android and iOS. If after you record your idea you want to turn your voice to text, then you might want to consider the application for both Android & iOS called Rev Voice Recorder. (www.rev.com). If you are taking notes with a pencil and piece of paper and want to digitize it, I recommend that you take a picture with your smart phone, or scan it with an application such as Genius Scan, then save the document to either a folder on your desktop or laptop, or just upload it to a cloud-based system like Evernote. I personally use Evernote for my entire note taking, and I find it quite efficient and useful. (www.evernote.com)

Secondly, if you like to draw, sketch out the thought without worrying about how good it will look. When we initially manifest a new idea, it is not about how great it looks on paper; it is all about recording and capturing the idea.

Frequently, ideas will spark during a stream of consciousness with a list of thoughts almost as if they were clumped together. When this happens, write your heart out to capture all of these great ideas. Again caution: what comes in through your intuition will evaporate into the ether. That's not to say it won't reappear at some point, but many of your ideas will be lost if you don't immediately record them. So record your ideas in the quickest and simplest ways possible for you.

Practice Silence

Lastly, capturing your ideas is about preparing and readying your consciousness to allow access to your soul's calling. I have spoken about contemplation, meditation, and mindfulness—but I have not addressed the simple technique of *silence*.

Silencing the body and mind, and getting into a vibratory space to tune into our soul's intuition is not something that requires a regular practice of meditation or mindfulness. Although, I would recommend it, for you will probably attain frequent access to your intuition if you regularly practice these techniques.

One way of getting into a state of silence requires that you use a simple technique of emptying the contents of your brain on paper. Write out everything that is on your mind.

David Allen, the author of *Making it all Work: Winning at the Game of Work and the Business of Life*, refers to this as the "Brain Dump." He says that our brain only has so much RAM and that most of the time it is full, and frequently it's hard to access the data because the RAM is full. He states, *"If you have a useful idea, leaving it in your head causes a part of your internal computer to try to keep track of it, that diminishes to some degree your mind's ability to process other thoughts because it's expending energy trying not to lose the first one."*

I like to practice what I have coined the *Silence Solution*. It's important to have our mind be as empty as possible before we attempt the *Silence Solution*. If our mind is empty, we will have full access to our intuition. By creating highly favorable conditions, we'll have access to new ideas that can manifest into our dreams of new products, services, and other ways to help our world.

The Silence Solution works like this:

1. Find a comfortable chair or sofa to sit in, but don't get too relaxed.

2. Ensure that other people won't interrupt you.

3. Turn off all electronic devices including your smart phone.

4. Have a paper and pencil by your side.

5. Observe the room or location you are in, even if your choice is to go outdoors.

6. Watch and listen for any movements or sounds.

7. Sit with your eyes open, and just listen—do this for fifteen minutes. (The first time you try the *Silence Solution* this will seem like an eternity.)

8. Close your eyes for fifteen minutes.

9. Create a mantra you can say to yourself silently. It could be something like, *"Universe please open up my consciousness to receive your many blessings."* This is your mantra so make it special for you.

10. After fifteen minutes, open your eyes slowly. Take time to listen and observe what is around you. Pause, then put the pencil and paper in your hand and write what comes to your mind.

I've never found a time when applying the *Silence Solution* that I didn't come up with a new thought or ideas that could change the way I do business or approach a new customer or build a better relationship.

David Whyte, author of *Crossing the Unknown Sea: Work as a Pilgrimage of Identity* says,

"Silence is the soul's break for freedom."

How to Transform Your Ideas into Reality

Transforming your ideas into reality can be a long journey. As you can see by the *Hacking the Gap* process on page 42 there are many steps, and while some steps you might be able to skip, usually it is best to work through all eight of them. These steps have been tested, not only by myself, but with my clients and the results are quite astounding.

It is not about "hacking steps" in the process; it is about *Hacking the Gap*. This means to find the shortest distance between the points with the least amount of resistance, while personally growing and becoming the best you can become. Tapping into your human potential and finding ways to keep doing that on a consistent basis will be the secret to manifesting your ideas into reality.

And again, the first step into manifesting your ideas into reality will be to *articulate the idea on paper as well as to be able to vocally describe your idea to anyone with whom you speak about your new idea.*

This step is of utmost importance—for the act of being able to articulate your idea allows you to solidify the idea into your consciousness. You are creating a vivid mental picture that is stable and fortified, through your personal conviction.

While you need to do this first step, I encourage you to have an open mind about other ideas that you might hear from associates, colleagues, and others. These ideas can have a positive influence on helping you refine your insight. Remember, the creation of ideas and manifesting them into products, services, or something that could help millions of people is not just about "you." It is a collective process where you stimulate streams of consciousness and ideas from others who contribute to your idea. Whether we're talking about a product or service, musical creation, or art in any form, *it does take a village* to elevate and develop your idea before you can properly send these ideas out into the world. Your "primary idea" will foster discussions, and new thoughts that beget grander ideas that can help make your service or product better.

A simple word to remember is "*refinement.*" I have rarely seen an insight go directly to production without some refinement. We are constantly refining our idea to a point where we are satisfied with the final product or service.

Once we have refined our idea, as well as listened and adopted ideas from others into our product or service, we can complete the visualization process. Visualizing is where the product or service is in our mind's eye. Then it gets converted to a drawing or document to conceptualize whatever it is we want to develop. When it exists on paper, in a drawing, or maybe even a prototype we have crafted, we can show our idea to others.

This process of taking our ideas from visualization in our minds eye to a design and then to that of a prototype is how we manifest our ideas into physical form and birth our new ideas. Having something to hold onto is so important to spring boarding our energy and inspire us to keep moving forward, even if it seems daunting. I personally know this process so well from the days of co-creating a positive role model doll for kids called Wanna-Be.

Developing twelve different role model dolls might sound simple, but it couldn't be further from the truth. Our team had to go from a cute drawing on paper to manifesting a prototype made in China with parts that were accessed from all around the world. Our Wanna-Be dolls had hair imported from Italy and eyes that were made in Germany, and a body that was created from molds that were made in Taiwan, then assembled in China with the final boxing completed here in the United States. Quite a feat to say the least, but when we see our dream start to come together, it infuses us with energy, and inspires us to move forward even though our world will be filled with many long nights, demands on our time and time away from our family.

This experience taught me so much, and was just one of many experiences I have had in developing products or services that gives me the credibility to speak with you about the *Hacking the Gap* process.

Mindset Applications to Hack the Gap of Frequency/Recording and Capturing Your Ideas

If you want to improve the frequency in *Hacking the Gap* and develop lots of new ideas, then you need to place yourself into an environment that is optimal for accessing your intuition, thus leading to aha moments.

The following is a short list of ways you can invoke *Hacking the Gap* to sustain the flow of ideas:

- Always keep a paper and pencil with you or by your bedside. You need to be able to record ideas that come to you.

- Practice the *Silence Solution* which is a daily practice of giving yourself thirty minutes to practice the eight steps outlined above in this chapter.

- Do "Brain Dumps" frequently. Brain dumps can be done anytime, but are especially effective before entering the *Silence Solution* sessions. Getting in the habit of doing "Brain Dumps" is a good habit of keeping your mind clear, allowing you to access your intuition at any time.

- The world is always calling you and distracting you from being in silence. Turn off electronic devices, smart phones, radio, television, and computers. Take a break one day a week if that is possible. Believe me people can wait. There is nothing so important that you can't take a "retreat day" from the phones and emails.

- Learn to take cues from nature and your surrounds. Look for signs, that you are on the right track (or perhaps off track). They are all around. Interpret the meaning of those signs. You are being guided at all times by the Universe. By deciphering the code of a soaring hawk or the appearance of a dolphin close to shore, you may be that much closer to *Hacking the Gap* of your brilliance.

- Do whatever you need to do to eliminate stress in your life. Stress is the single biggest killer of great ideas. Exercise, meditate, listen to music—whatever you need to or "not do" to remove the stress.

INSPIRATION
Knowing It's Right

CHAPTER 4

INSPIRATION:
Realizing Your Knowings, Not Your Beliefs

*"The true basis of religion is not belief, but intuitive experience.
Intuition is the soul's power of knowing God.
To Know what religion is all about, one must know God."*
—Paramahansa Yogananda

During phone conversations with my good friend Jerry Dillard, he will focus on our understanding of our knowings versus our beliefs. He spends hours reading and studying a cross section of spiritual content. He often quotes from the New Testament that we are better benefited by being *"of the world"* and not *"in the world."*

How you choose to interpret this quote is dependent upon your perspective. The meaning for me, *is to live life from that of a spiritual being,* and not from the perspective of always seeking more or wanting more. While a material world is part of what we all live in, we can't get caught in the ego's trap of seeking more at the expense of others. Our purpose should be to live a life focused on helping and serving—not riding rough shod over our fellow human beings.

We often believe that material possession will make us happy. I've learned from the conversations with my friend, and from my own reflections, the importance of being able to differentiate between our beliefs and our knowings. When we are in the world, we have strong propensities to have lots of worldly possessions. I am not professing that this is a wrong thing, but when we shift our perspective and look at the world by how much we can contribute and give, the possessions are no longer a strong attraction. Knowings are from the soul and the urges we feel when we participate in activities that serve others.

Beliefs are constructs of our mind and the summation of experience we have had in life. They are formulated from facts, data, and experiences we collect from the physical world.

They are certainties of the mind, but are not certainties of our spirit and soul. We formulate beliefs in our mind, and they create the world that we live in and our perceptions of reality. These beliefs are formulated from facts and data that to us are true, or from erroneous information and facts that for some reason we still believe to be true. Beliefs form our realities and what we stand for. The beliefs that we have can lead us to taking a stance for something that we have strong convictions about, so much so that our beliefs have created wars, poverty, injustices, and all kinds of deplorable acts against humanity.

We are always going to have our personal beliefs and differences of opinion, and these differences are what create a dynamic world and make it a very interesting place to live. Yet our beliefs are subject to change. If someone or something can convince us differently, we will *change our mind*—this phrase is used frequently when people have a change in their belief. This means that the evidence and how it was presented was overwhelmingly convincing enough to get us to alter and change how we stand on a particular position.

"I WILL NEVER GET OFF THIS ISLAND!"

So if beliefs are subject to change based upon us revising our opinions or formulating a new perspective, that makes our beliefs tenuous and pliable—agreed? Think about it...how many of your beliefs about something that you thought were "gospel" or "fact" were later changed when you received additional information to persuade you otherwise? We have beliefs on subjects varying from relationships, money, world affairs, politics, business opportunities, and spirituality and the list is endless.

Beliefs rarely change in a moment; they are revised over time, with time being one of the factors that has a tremendous influence on our beliefs.

I have countless examples of beliefs being changed, but one example that comes to mind is the public opinions and differing beliefs on global warming.

Al Gore had been researching global warming since 1981 and after his presidential bid in 2000 he returned to his passion, giving numerous presentations. He formed "The Climate Reality Project" in 2005, and released his documentary film, *An Inconvient Truth*, in 2006, which won two Academy awards. His predictions created lots of controversy at the time—some scientists defied what he was saying, and other scientists supported the fact that global warming was a real thing. Needless to say that since his first presentations in 2005, our world has been experiencing the real effects of global warming, in my personal opinion.

International governments are working to eradicate the effects of global warming. So has your belief changed since 2005? I know that my belief has been strengthened and supported by the scientific facts. I am more concerned about the issue of global warming than I have ever been. I have altered my lifestyle; and this change was significantly influenced by my convictions becoming stronger over the years since my first awareness of global warming. I have cut down on my commutes and meet people on line with video chats. I've embraced the use of hybrid vehicles by driving a Toyota Prius, and as a matter of fact, I recently just purchased, my third Toyota Prius since my awareness that global warming is a world-wide issue. I limit my air travel miles, and recycle everything in an effort to reduce my personal CO_2 footprint and reduce emissions.

The example about global warming illustrates that our beliefs do change over time and are influenced by a rise in new technologies, human consciousness, greater awareness of the issues and concerns for humanity, and our socially responsible politicians and thought leaders. Politicians, business leaders, and the general public are having discussions daily about how global warming is affecting the lives of people worldwide. When an issue such as global warming starts to affect our life and threatens our existence on our planet, we pay attention quickly—unless we've had our heads in the sand.

Other factors that alter our beliefs are life-threating illness, divorce, bankruptcy, and numerous other circumstances that are usually met with resistance. "This can't be happening to me" are the words out of many people's mouths when something adverse happens. Then often they spend years in resistance of the event, fighting it all the way to their grave. The best advice I can offer when you are provided with the opportunity that adversity presents in your life is to accept the bad things that occur as wonderful learning lessons and alter your life accordingly. I realize that acceptance of whatever challenge you may be facing can be difficult, but believe me the alternative of being resistant is worse.

If you were a smoker prior to a heart attack, good chances are that you reformulated your beliefs about how good that cigarette was for you. If you gained thirty pounds over the years, as I personally have, you are now looking at what effects the extra thirty pounds is having on your health and formulating new habits and beliefs about food, exercise, and nutrition.

We pay more attention to the things that have the biggest impact on our lives. It's just a fact. We refer to them as *wake-up* calls for a reason; most importantly, because they are bringing a heightened level of awareness to the beliefs that no longer serve us. We all carry around beliefs that do not serve and do not contribute to our highest and best good. As we conduct our lives we can learn to ask the right questions, especially during adversity, so that the actions we choose are working in our highest and best good.

Again, understanding the difference between your knowings and beliefs is important. Beliefs can change, and are temporary. In contrast, a "knowing" is not temporary or subject to change. As defined by Webster's dictionary, it is to:

"Know, comprehend, understand, imply being aware of meanings. To know is to be aware of something as a fact or truth."

One of the major differences is that knowing is *truth* for you. Truth is a verifiable indisputable fact. It does not have to be an indisputable truth for another person; this is your knowing not someone else's. When we stand "in our knowing," we are 100% certain that this is true, right and correct. We will not be convinced otherwise. It is impossible to argue with a person who has a strong "knowing." When we have a "knowing," we will defend our facts or principles no matter what. Our knowings become part of our character. We express them in how we live our life, and we exemplify this behavior to everyone we meet in the world.

An example of a knowing that has been the longest debate of all time is of the existence of a higher power—God, Allah, Buddha, or whatever you want to call your higher power. We either believe in the existence of this higher power or we don't.

If you are an atheist or agnostic, then the existence of a higher power or God is no part of your life. If you are spiritual or religious, the existence of a higher power has been something that you usually have been taught from a young age by being exposed to one religion or another. You don't necessarily have to have had a personal experience with your higher power and many times the existence of God or a higher power has not been proven to you through personal experiences with God.

Wars have been fought and countless people have died defending their positions about the existence of a "higher power," be it Allah, Buddha, Jesus, or whatever deity they have had a personal "knowing" about.

Do people change religious "beliefs"? You bet. Do people change religious and spiritual knowings?—Absolutely not. They will keep these "knowings" until the day they die, and if you believe in reincarnation they might keep their knowings for lifetimes.

What does all this have to do with being inspired?

The origin of the word *inspiration* is an immediate influence of God. It means the process of being mentally stimulated to do or feel something, especially to do something creative.

Inspiration is a very important element in the *Hacking the Gap* process. At this point in the development of our creative ideas, we are being inspired to move forward, take action, and tell the world our amazing story. We are so certain—we have a *knowing*—that our idea is worth telling the world about. We want to have everyone hear our story. We want to express our idea and get it out to the world. In the inspiration stage, we get a boost of energy from inside that is beyond any runner's high. In my humble opinion, we are being guided by a divine power and it is time to "go for it." It is time to take the risk, be bold, and step out of our comfort zone.

Your soul has been speaking with you and you must listen to the guidance. Don't ignore the calling.

This is not the time to question our ideas or have others tell us that our ideas will not succeed. This is the time to reinforce our plans, listen to people that want to support us and provide us with encouragement and guidance. The inspiration state undoubtedly is the point where there is *wind beneath your wings,* and you are soaring and absolutely nothing can stop you.

The Being and Doing Conundrum

I have spent a good portion of my life "doing." They say if you want to get something done ask a busy person. Well, that busy person is me. I get asked to help people manifest their dreams. This same experience might be the case for many of you reading this book. It took me years to understand that a good mix between "being" and "doing" is more important to my personal happiness and overall well-being.

I now understand that the "being" is a state of consciousness that was calling to me and asking for me to pay attention. My being was longing to be nurtured and cared for; it was the side of me that I had forgotten. However, as painful as being in the state of "doing" was for a large part of my existence, it certainly prepared me to be a good teacher to others about the importance of balancing this life between their "being" and "doing." Being driven without a balance of living our life on purpose and giving ourselves time to just be can produce tremendous anxiety, fear, and misunderstanding about what the world has really bestowed upon us to experience.

When we are constantly "doing," we miss out on the many pleasures of being a spiritual being in a physical world. We are so focused on the goal line and not the learning line, we gloss over all the great experiences of life that lead up to the achievement of our goals.

This quote by Henry David Thoreau articulates my point well:

> **"What you get by achieving your goals is not as import-**
> **ant as what you become by achieving your goals."**

"Being" is about becoming. It is about taking the time to observe who you are becoming by going for the stretch goal. It is the person you are molded into as a result of *going for it* regardless of the outcome.

Yet, we are drawn on a daily basis to become "doing" beings. Almost all of you reading this book have a job or go somewhere to work for your living. The questions I have are: Does the job you engage in provide you with joy and meaning, or it is just a job? The job of an entrepreneur in large part is one of doing. Those are the activities that many companies want from us because it keeps the "corporate machine" moving. It keeps our small- to medium-sized businesses pulsating with life.

The real creative pulse comes from the heart of our being. It is *why we do what we do*; it is our creative energy that drives that new idea that gets turned into a new product or service that can change the whole world.

I encourage you—I emplore you—please do not spend the largest portion of your time on this planet "doing." Develop a healthy balance between "being and "doing"—trust me you will feel better, and the world will benefit from your "being." You will have fewer health challenges, your attitude will be revived, your perception of the world will be expansive, and the people and your relationships will be greatly improved.

If you are interested in reading more on this topic I recommend a wonderful book by a friend of mind on the conundrum of being and doing and learn to become more creative. The author is Barnett Bain and the book is entitled *The Book of Doing and Being—Rediscover Creativity in Life, Love, and Work*. He has a great comment about structured imaging:

> "The reason we tend to draw inside the line is because we have inherited those lines and perspectives. We are products of our families, peer groups, schools, entertainment streams and religions. We are shaped by the movies, TV shows, songs, news bites, stories and art forms offered to us by other people-expression of the tragedies and triumphs that seem to dictate the reach of our imagination. Some call this structured imagining, which is our unconscious adoption of other people's thinking, feeling, beliefs, and values. We are mostly unaware that we have acquired a hand-me-down worldview."

Imagination, Inspiration & Innovation the Magic Elixirs

Albert Einstein said,

> "Imagination is more important than knowledge. For knowledge is limited, whereas imagination embraces

the entire world, stimulating progress, giving birth
to evolution."

Notice that in the *Hacking the Gap* process diagram you did not
find "imagination" on the wheel. I didn't purposely leave it out;
and it is certainly a crucial part of the whole process of creativity.
For me imagination is ignited by the ability to get in touch with
our intuition. If I can help you access your intuition more frequently, the by-product is a massive increase in your imagination.

In essence, our intuition sparks imagination, which leads to
"great ideas." This in turn leads us on the path of exploration
toward innovation. While there are several steps in between in the
Hacking the Gap process the intent is that we learn new ways of
experiencing the ability to reduce the time spent between the steps.
Our energy and the flow of inspiration is elevated by the progress
we are making toward the achievement of our dream and goals.

I believe that on the journey of the creative process from inspiration we move to the "incubation stage," then to the "ignition
stage" before we reach "innovation." Innovation is the creating and
building of that idea into a product, service or socially responsible
idea that will save the world.

While in the incubation stage, we are working through the
"kinks," allowing our ideas to develop into something that our
team believes can improve, enhance, or revolutionize a way in
which something is currently being done or a completely new way
of doing something in the world.

Innovation is the "act or process of introducing a new idea, devices
or methods." The key word in this definition is "introducing." At
this stage we bring our product, service, or method to the world
through the process of testing and refining our product or service.

We are not quite ready to launch that "new something." We are gaining feedback, and making any modifications to our products or invention. This is a big step, and one that cannot be taken lightly: for during the innovation stage we are proving if our product is worthy by our prospective customers.

Product development lifecycles differ from industry to industry. Some can be as short as a month, while others like the pharmaceutical industry can take years as in bringing a new drug to the market, which is protracted due to the massive testing requirement by the FDA (Food & Drug Administration).

No matter what our development lifecycle, testing requirements, or whatever you go through to validate your product or service, remember the inspiring ideas that originated that idea. Tap your intuition to gain an insight, then move to an idea. Be inspired and have a "knowing" that it is right. Having the conviction to move it into the incubation phase is an amazing process.

> **BEWARE: Negative thoughts, uncertainty, doubt, fear, and an inability to tap into your source of inspiration will kill great ideas.**

Sustaining Your Inspiration Quotient

The inspiration quotient is the factor that allows us to sustain a high level of "juice" about ourselves, our world, and the product and or service we are developing.

The common denominators that are part of the inspiration quotient are: *awareness, flow, openness, renewal, reward, fulfillment, joy, happiness, doing, being, belonging, community, thinking big, boldness, and support.* If you are finding that these words resonate with you and you are able to hold on to your enthusiasm for the project you are working on, then you are probably in the *hacking the gap* state.

Remaining inspired requires that you tap into your *soul's signal*— the voice that speaks to you with encouragement and informs you to keep moving in spite of possible adversity or setbacks. Inspiration will heal any negative emotions, depression, or fears and it allows you to stay in the flow.

If you want to remain in this state of awareness so that your inspired consciousness overrides the thousands of "negative" thoughts that can creep into your mind, spend more time reminding yourself that you are the instrument of creativity, that you have been chosen to bring this idea to the world, and that this idea is needed to support your organization, company, or socially just cause. This idea needs to be birthed. You (and your team) have been given the responsibility to make it happen. Your conviction and dedication need to be unwavering. You must *know* that the product, service, method, or idea is right—the time is right and the world is ready.

Sustaining the inspiration quotient can be tough. You will be met with resistance but you must forge through any and all resistance the world sends your way to manifest your ideas into something great.

Inertia—The Killer of Inspiration and What To Do About It

By definition inertia is "the tendency to do nothing or to remain unchanged." Yes, inertia will take hold; it will get a grip and do everything imaginable to keep you from the manifestation of your great idea. Shiny objects will distract you and move you from the ultimate development of your idea. Inertia literally is the killer of "bright ideas."

I encourage you to continue to take small steps toward your goal and manifestation of your idea into physical form. Small steps daily are what provide the fuel and inspiration to see the finish line. Manifesting your idea into reality is the same as taking steps toward a goal. You have to break it down into manageable actions. It must hold value and meaning, or you will loose interest.

I recently conducted an interview with Dr. Edwin Locke, one of the foremost experts on goal setting and task performance. He stated, *"Proximal or short-term goals are required to attain long-term goals. The future is a potential and it is not real: short-term goals provide you with the confidence to reach your long-term goals.* So remember to break down your goals and intentions into subtasks.

Author Richard L. Draft, in his book *The Executive and the Elephant*, says

> **"Spend time each morning to set your explicit imple-mentation intentions. Implementation intention can be thought of as defining the specific step-by step activities that will lead to your goal or desired outcome. Your inner elephant is more likely to move ahead if it can see each tiny, concrete step."**

It's important not to overthink your project. I am sure you are aware of the statement "paralysis by analysis." So many projects are stopped because of stinking thinking. Just put one foot in front of the other and take small steps toward a successful completion of a phase or element of your product, service, or idea. You must see incremental "wins." The concept of incremental wins is an import-ant psychological element that juices you to continue on.

A great analogy is when you start a weight loss program, and you get on the scale each week and you see a reduction in your weight by a few pounds. Those measurements give you incentive to continue on with the new habits that are resulting in the weight loss.

Building an idea, service or product is not easy, and it usually is not simple either. But that is no excuse not take on something that is a hard-to-reach goal, provided your product, service, or idea is driven by your personal purpose to make a difference. This is your way to make a great contribution to the world. Identify the concrete steps that will provide you incentive to keep going.

If your idea is being inspired by your soul and driven by that voice inside that inspires you to continue on, then you know it is right. Please do not give up. Don't pitch in the towel at the first sign of any obstacle.

As Thomas Edison said,

> **"Many of life's failures are people who did not realize how close they were to success when they gave up."**

Steven Pressfield writes about our enemy in his book *The War of Art: Break Through the Blocks and Win Your Inner Creative Battles,* "Resistance is the most toxic force on the planet. It is the root of more unhappiness than poverty, disease, and erectile dysfunction. To yield to Resistance deforms our spirit. It stuns us and makes us less than we were born to be. If you believe in God (and I do), you must declare Resistance evil, for it prevents us from achieving the life God intended when He endowed each of us with our own unique genius."

Mindset Applications for
Hacking the Gap of Inspiration

- If you listen to music, then listen to more. Noting can be quite as inspiring as jamming to your favorite tunes. Let the music take you to another world, one where you are released from all your cares and obligations.

- Practice doing brain dumps of all that stuff that is in your head. Use this application to get your "to-dos" out of your RAM (random accessory memory) and on to paper. You cannot do anything if you're just thinking about your to-dos. They all require action and that likely requires that you write an email, make a phone call, or set up a meeting. No matter what it is, don't let it take up the creative space in your consciousness.

- Who is the most inspiring person you know? Write down their name. (Your mother, father, Gandhi, whomever.) If you can speak with them, then call immediately. If it is someone famous and you don't believe you can reach them or they are dead, then listen to a podcast, video, or whatever they have created that inspires you. The key is to soak your consciousness with their essence so that you are so inspired you take action.

- Are you part of a mastermind group, or any group of like-minded people that give you inspiration? If not join one, or create a group of your own if you are not part of a group. Being in community is a must; you can't go the creative process alone. $1 + 1 = 3$. There is amazing synergy from the process of sharing your ideas, thoughts, and challenges with others that care and want to help you become successful.

- I am not certain where you are in the development cycle of your idea, product, or service, but taking time to "chill" is always a great way to get inspired. Commune with nature. Get away from your work and take a break. Plan at least three days away from your office and your day-to-day responsibilities every quarter to rejuvenate and reset. You will find that this "away time" will get your engines reengaged and inspired ideas and breakthroughs will occur much more quickly. This is one of the best ways to assist you in "Hacking the Gap."

INCUBATION
Maturation Process

CHAPTER 5

INCUBATION:
The Evolution of Your Insights, Ideas, and Inspiration

"Generating ideas is not a problem. Incubation is. Acceleration is."
—Ruth Gunther McGrath, American strategic management scholar
and professor of management at the Columbia Business School

Incubation is one of the steps in the *Hacking the Gap* process which volumes have been written about and debated by business thought leaders.

Author Eric Weiner in his book, *The Geography of Genius: A Search for the World's Most Creative Places From Ancient Athens to Silicon Valley,* says,

> "The creative act always requires a stepping back. It's called the incubation period. The incubation period— one of the four phases of creativity—is when you're not consciously thinking of a problem, and you're letting it marinate. So this is why you hear time and again,

people saying they had that "Eureka" moment in the
bath, like Archimedes, or in the shower, or while going
for a walk or in a coffeehouse."

During the incubation phase, you will find that many questions
will arise, many which will be supporting. Other thoughts will
come forth validating the concept, idea, product, or service. Take
time to include other people in the overall creative process. It
doesn't matter if you are a big company incubating an idea or
a first timer. Solicit feedback from people you trust—and who
genuinely want to support you in your endeavors. All feedback be
it positive or negative is just feedback. The feedback only becomes
positive or negative by you responding to the feedback and becoming emotionally charged. It's a lot like writing a book, then editing
the book, and then giving the book to others for feedback. If you
choose to make every change suggested by readers, the book would
never be completed.

Be prepared for criticism and cynicism because people are there
to test us. Even though we might have the "knowing" because this
idea is our baby, many others don't "know" what we inherently
understand about our idea. People may disapprove and shoot holes
in the concepts. This is a good thing and a necessary part of the
creative process. This helps us see areas of improvement that were
hidden from us because we were too close to gain objectivity. No
one said the creation of a product or service was going to be simple
or easy for that matter, but this is a necessary element to developing
a marketable item.

The four phases of creativity—*preparation, incubation, illumination, and verification*—can be the most protracted of all the steps
in the *Hacking the Gap* process. Don't get discouraged by the
amount of time it takes to go through these steps. Validation is the

proof of concept, and this requires time, persistence, and lots of diligent effort to complete.

I remember the months of meetings, and the time it took our team to develop a cloud-based software system called Digital Seed. During the creative process, I spent hours developing the concept with many iterations of what we believed it would look like as well as the user experience we were attempting to create. Many series of iterations were created to ultimately get to the beta. We then took the idea and a prototype to a small subset of people to get their opinions and feedback. The feedback was not always overwhelmingly positive, and that was a good thing because we wanted users to have a great experience, especially when it comes to navigating software.

The illumination of the idea developed through our master plan and private placement memorandum document that was created to articulate the idea to investors. I didn't have any success raising money, but regardless of the interest I decided to proceed forward with the project using my own investment.

Our nimble team worked feverishly to develop the first working beta. Remember what I said about estimating that your projects will take twice as long and cost twice as much money, well that is what happened with Digital Seed, and unfortunately I ran out of money. This is the worst thing that can happen to an entrepreneur with a great idea. The idea and all the investment disappeared into the ether, but the lessons and insights I gained were priceless. If you want to learn more about this venture, check out the website at www.digital-seed.com.

Testing, retesting, tweaking and finalizing so many elements of the "design" takes patience. Risk becomes a calculated risk during the creative phase. As we become clearer, focused, and committed, our soul speaks with to us more frequently and encourages us to stay the path. Fear becomes a distant factor, and we become the most committed we have ever been in our life to completing our special projects.

The Chaos Factor

As you evolve during the creative process and move through the four phases, realize that chaos is something that inevitability happens along the way.

Examples from my own personal experiences vary from prototype parts that were manufactured incorrectly, molds that needed adjusting, and coding that was written and re-written. No matter what the example, things are bound to go wrong, and when it does you can spin into a chaotic state of consciousness. Your mind immediately rushes to the lost time, financial overruns, and fear of never completing the project. Chaos and mistakes are part of the process; please take them in stride. Plan for them, because they are going to happen!

When we are in the incubation phase of the creative process, we might find evidence that requires immediate attention, and modification to the invention or idea.

One such chaotic event occurred around a trademark issue with the Wanna-Be doll. Someone in Canada stated that they had the trademark on Wanna-Be. This kind of possible trademark infringement usually comes on a day when you least expect it via registered mail. It is called a cease and desist. Challenges like these drain your time, energy, and pocketbook.

In this incident I flew to Canada and made an offer to purchase the trademark rights from a woman in Canada for the product we were attempting to develop. This person had a similar name and trademark that *was not in use* as defined by the trademark and patient office.

Incidences like this one could have been prevented if we would have bought the rights initially or changed the name of the company and product. Our decision was not based on the fact that we had not researched the other person's filing; it was a *calculated risk* based on the fact that the other trademark was out of the United States. What you must realize is that some people in foreign countries will "hijack" companies for money. I later found this out from our attorney—that certain countries don't have treaties with the United States which allows for this kind of behavior.

Trademark fights cause stress, create sleepless nights and bring on "chaos" in anyone's life and organization. One day you don't have a care in the world, then all of a sudden you open the mail or get a phone call and are thrust into a battle for your life.

If this happens, persistence, fortitude, and a fighting mental spirit are necessary. Stay the path, and go the distance with what you know; you will find out that most of the time your "knowing" was worth fighting for.

One way to avoid chaos is to do a trademark and patent search early in the process. Getting a good trademark and patient attorney is worth the investment. They will guide you through the maze of paperwork and will do the research for you. Be warned, if you do take your idea this far and you decide to secure the services of a trademark attorney, prepare yourself to invest a considerable sum of money.

It's not easy to let go of something we are so invested in, especially when you know you have not done anything wrong. Don't just take it lying down. Stand up and take the appropriate actions to hang on to your dream. If, however, it does become necessary for you to "let go," just know that this act is in your best interest. Good will come of it.

Thriving in the Midst of Chaos

Chaos is an interesting phenomenon. We are all subject to it, and when it happens, it simulates the effects of a tornado in our life. The interesting part is that from chaos comes order, a new order that previously did not exist before the chaos struck. I certainly don't enjoy the chaotic experience, but after it happens and we clean up our act, things are usually better than before the incident.

Our minds often breed chaos as well. As we are receiving ideas, the ping ponging of these ideas in our mind can be chaotic. At times, our minds are loaded with thoughts and ideas whirling around that don't make much sense—then something magical happens; they converge into that *one thought* that has meaning and significance for us. This idea becomes the foundation of our creation—we *know* when it's right. We can trust in what we have been given because we know our soul has taken a role in the development of the idea. When this happens our soul is insistent; it doesn't let up, it hounds us (in a good way); it wakes us in the middle of the night—not with worry, but excitement, as it calls us to be the vehicle for the manifestation of a new idea.

Our role is to become the receptacle and to assist the Universe in the creation of the co-created idea into reality. We are just the receiver, the chosen one to bring this new idea to the world. However, please do not take your new role lightly; you have an obligation to see this through no matter what happens. Being the person chosen to manifest this idea is one of the fastest ways to accelerate your own *personal growth,* allowing you to reach the highest levels of *human potential.*

Elizabeth Gilbert, in *Big Magic: Creative Living Beyond Fear,* says,

> "Trust in the miraculous truth that new and marvelous ideas are looking for human collaborators every single day. Ideas of every kind are constantly galloping toward us, constantly passing through us, constantly trying to get our attention. Let them know you're available. And for heaven's sake, try not to miss the next one."

Sowing Your Seeds, the Sprouting of Your Personal Growth

Remember, by definition *Hacking the Gap* is "the shortest distance between two points with the least amount of resistance, designed to forge your personal growth and human potential."

There is however another term that you should become familiar with and that is Gapology—the methodologies, processes, procedures, and applications that you avail yourself of in life and business that assist you in finding, exploring, utilizing and implementing solutions to reach your goals and dreams.

The incubation stage will test you and the development of your idea by the outside world on what you know is the truth. Negative self-talk reaffirming your uncertainty will certainly raise its ugly head attempting you to abandon the development and manifestation of your idea. We all have heard these voices before, not only from our own ego, but also from the egos of friends, family, and associates. Whenever you are birthing an idea and it has evolved to the incubation stage, you will be tested, personally, professionally, spiritually, emotionally, and mentally.

If you have anchored the "knowing" that your idea is going to make a difference and contribution to the world, then you are being guided by your soul and a divine power to overcome the distractions, uncertainty, doubt, and fear. Remember who you really are, what you are made of, and the personal character you possess to carry through with the manifestation of the idea.

Wisdom from Other Innovators

I have conducted over 600 interviews with authors and thought leaders on personal growth, wellness, business, mastery, and spirituality. The distillation of this immense body of work can be summarized in ten (10) salient points:

- You must believe in yourself and have self-confidence in who and what you stand for.

- You have to remain persistent in light of the challenges you will encounter.

- You must learn from your mistakes, and don't repeat the mistakes twice.

- Fear and doubt should be silenced to allow for the birth of a new idea.

- Set proximal and incremental goals, and focus on your vision.

- Have a purpose, and live by your purpose—allow that to guide everything you do all day long.

- Your personal happiness is the most important emotion to keep you inspired. Do whatever you do to bring joy, peace, and fulfillment to your mission.

- Don't be attached to your idea. Know that life is impermanent and so might be your idea. It could morph, change, or take new form.

- Learn to be like water and flow with whatever comes to you. Resistance is futile and only arises to keep you from taking action.

- Connect with the people that are your support structure. A community of support is so important to remain in the "creative collective."

If you take from this list and apply the ideas mentioned, you will find that your journey from intuition to innovation and beyond can become a joyful and pleasant experience.

My goal for you is that you have the least amount of resistance along your journey and experience the greatest amount of joy and happiness. If this is to occur, you must keep reminding yourself about who you really are, what you are made of, and *why* you chose to do this now.

Why has this idea birthed itself at this juncture of your life? Why am I being called to be bold, step out of my comfort zone? How did this spark of my inspiration from my soul, that "intuitive sense" finally connect the dots and awaken new possibilities from within me?

The truth about this new idea is that it was always "within" you. You just needed a synchronistic set of circumstances to have the confidence to birth your idea. These circumstances revolve around your personal growth and human potential, tapping deeply into the creative energy that was waiting to *connect the dots* from your subconscious mind—to bring forth the convergence of thoughts, ideas, and patterns that finally needed a place for expression.

You become the expression of these ideas that merge into one, and when you share your idea with others who are supportive, that idea evolves further because you are tapping into the "collective consciousness" that propels that idea into perfect manifestation.

Project Development Life Cycles

I don't need to pontificate about project development life cycles. It's only important to note that in the incubation stage there are four phases that you will go through before you reach the implementation stage.

The first is to look at the **requirements** of your project. What are the imperative elements that need to be considered before you begin?

The second is the **design** itself. Do you have a complete design? Does it need modification or changes before you begin development?

The third is **development**—what components are required to develop your product, service, or idea. Do you need funding? Have you purchased the components to create the prototype? Do you need to outsource various elements of the development?

The fourth stage is **testing**—Do you need to test your idea with the general public? Will you test this in a lab first? How many times will you test the product or service? How much feedback do you want from testers before you choose to launch?

I have intentionally only mentioned these stages without going into depth because entire books are written about product development life cycles. Keep one thing in perspective and that is you will need project management software to assist you in keeping track of your developments on the project. You will be tracking people, vendors, and resources and this requires that you hire a project manager, or in the initial stages of development that project manager might be you.

No matter what you choose to do, project management software is going to make the journey much easier. I have given references and links to several very good project management software systems in the reference section of the book.

At this juncture in the development of your idea, you are testing and retesting your idea to make sure it will work. Does it have all the components that will make it a better solution to the challenges people are faced with? Can your product or service help make the lives of the man or woman on the street easier and fulfill a need that they needs solving? The depth of development depends on the complexity of the project; some products and services can be tested quickly, while others require extensive testing and feedback.

There are so many combinations of your idea that can be tested to find the right link to make your product or service "just right." It can easily discourage even the committed creative inventor. Just remember this is a test; you are being tested to find out if you have what it takes to commit to manifesting your idea into reality. If this was easy everyone would be doing it, and they are not.

One out of 5,000 inventions have successful product launches. Only two products are launched out of every 3,000 ideas. Only 3,000 patents out of 1.5 million patents are commercially viable. One out of 100 patented products makes money. One out of a 100 make it. While these statistics might seem dismal remember yours just might be the one that does make it, and if it does not make it then you found one more way not to do something, and you can approach the development from a different perspective.

I know from personal experience. I was a king of product failures, and that's the reason I have credibility in assisting people in *Hacking the Gap* and realizing success at their project launch. My maturity at this game brought me to the understanding that the biggest culprit to success is *ego*. When you're the idea guy and or the inventor, you usually have lots of your ego tied up in whatever you are inventing.

A big ego will kill most products—dead.

Steve Jobs had a big ego and was known as a jerk by many people who worked for him. In blog post, entitled, "What It's Really Like Working with Steve Jobs," Glen Reid, who had previously worked at Adobe, NeXT and Apple, recounts the following:

> "Steve would draw a quick vision on the whiteboard, we'd go work on it for a while, bring it back, find out the ways in which it sucked, and we'd iterate, again and again and again. That's how it always went. Iteration. It's the key to design, really. Just keep improving it until you have to ship it."

> "He told me once that part of the reason he wanted to be CEO was so that nobody could tell him that he wasn't allowed to participate in the nitty-gritty of product design. He was right there in the middle of it. All of it. As a team member, not as CEO. He quietly left his CEO hat by the door, and collaborated with us. He was basically the Product Manager for all of the products I worked on, even though there eventually were other people with that title, who usually weren't allowed in the room."

So given this recount of one of the most famous innovators of all time, you can see how he worked. Steve Jobs may not have been the perfect guy to work for, but he was an amazing visionary and brilliant strategist. He possessed an unwavering commitment to everything he set his mind to doing. When he became involved in those incubation meetings with this team, people left their ego at the door—which is imperative to developing, testing, and creating wonderful products and services.

Mindset Applications for Hacking the Gap of Incubation and the Evolution of Your Insights, Ideas, and Inspirations

- Research your idea thoroughly. Spend time looking into your competition in the market, and know what problem you are solving for your customers and why they might want something like your new product or service.

- Know who is going to consume your service or product. Who is your avatar and what makes them tick?

- Give presentations to people once you have your idea fully developed. Spend this time getting prospective customer feedback and gathering information that could make your product or service better.

- Once you have gathered the data look inside yourself and listen to your soul's voice. What ideas will make your idea better, and only focus on those. Remember you will not be all things to all people, and there is no need to try.

- Try if possible to keep things simple. Some of the simplest ideas have made millions of dollars. Post-it notes over $29 billion in sales. Sara Blakely's Spanx undergarment for women, has made her a billionaire. Snuggie blanket has sold over 30 million.

- Some of your best ideas will spring out of "connecting the dots." Make sure you allow yourself the space and time to get in the "connecting the dots" space. Take more time to sit and think, and remember to do it in silence if possible.

- Many ideas are just more improved products or services of an existing product or service. What have you noticed that you believe needs changing or improving, and why? Ask your friends for feedback on your ideas.

- Think about who you might need to help you develop this new product or service. Are you going to need a prototype, if so who do you know who has the proper equipment to make it? Do you have a drawing or plan for the product? If so, share this with people that prototype new products.

- Have you thought about how much money will be required to develop your product or service? Do you have the money or are you going to need investors in your idea? Think through who might be your best investor(s) and why? What are their passions and do they align with your new product or service?

- Pull all the pieces of the development of your idea together, and think through every step of the development process. This is where the project management software will come in handy. Keep asking questions of everyone involved in the project, from vendors to friends and family. And again, solicit feedback as you progress with the development.

IGNITION
Managing Your Energy

CHAPTER 6

IGNITION:
Energy Management: Understanding and Identifying the Types of Energy

"Where focus goes energy flows."
—Tony Robbins

As we move forward with the development of our project and the various stages associated with its development, we need to consider the management of our energy. The birth of a new product or service requires that we carefully manage our personal energy. This is a very exciting time in our lives, and it is easy to get burned out due to working long hours with intense focus.

The closer we come to the implementation stage, the more energy we will utilize. Identifying and understanding what is happening is imperative so we don't dissipate our energy with unnecessary activities or distractions that absorb our mind power. We need to concentrate on our end product or service.

There are four types of energy that are being utilized during most of our waking hours and they are spiritual, mental, emotional and physical. Everyday, we are balancing our time moving from one type of energy to another.

Let me give you an example: when we wake up in the morning and we set our intentions and give gratitude, we are focused on the spiritual aspect of our life. Then when we go to the gym to engage in exercise, we are focused on our physical energy. If we do yoga, we are working with both the physical and the spiritual energies. If we have an argument with our spouse or a co-worker, the emotional energy kicks in and this can be the most draining use of our energy. I know that when I have a disagreement or my emotions are heightened by some incident, I personally feel drained emotionally and physically. Last, but not least is the use of our mental energy—when we are focused on a project or attempting to write a research paper or book, our mental energies are being maxed out.

Yet, we can see our projects to the end with concentration and determination. Charles Dickens said, *"I never could have done without the habits of punctuality, order, and diligence... the determination to concentrate myself on one subject at a time."* Dickens' quote says much about what it takes to stay focused. Ultimately, it's our disciplines and positive habits that will assist us in prevailing.

I know that in the fast paced world we live in today, it is easy to become distracted by all the messaging we are receiving through emails, texts, instant messaging and social media. We can only concentrate for short periods of time and that we lose our focus. It is necessary to eliminate the distractions.

In a newly released book, *The Distracted Mind*, Mark Gazzaley and Larry Rosen, explain that our brains are limited in their ability to pay attention.

> "We don't really multitask but rather switch rapidly between tasks. Distractions and interruptions, often technology-related—referred to by the authors as 'interference'—collide with our goal-setting abilities. We want to finish this paper/spreadsheet/sentence, but our phone signals an incoming message and we drop everything. Even without an alert, we decide that we 'must' check in on social media frequently."

Gazzaley and Rosen offer practical strategies, backed by science, to fight distraction. We can change our brains with meditation, video games, and physical exercise; we can change our behavior by planning our accessibility and recognizing our anxiety about being out of touch even briefly. They don't suggest that we give up our devices, but that we use them in a more balanced way."

If you ask someone who works outside in nature, for instance a gardener or construction worker, they will say they are tired, but their tired is from physical exertion. Work that exhausts us physically has a completely different impact on our body chemicals. I've often said, "I would rather be physically tired than mentally tired."

Here are the reasons for my statement, when we are physically working out, our bodies' chemistry releases endorphins, dopamine, and serotonin. All of these chemicals are designed to provide more energy and allow for us to have greater mental acuity.

On the other hand when we are mentally exhausted and stressed, our body releases cortisol and epinephrine. Both of these chemicals are linked to digestive disorders, heart disease, diabetes, weight gain, memory issues, and short attention span. I don't know about you, but stress has been the most challenging emotion that I have had to deal with. It is the culmination of our days' work where we have juggled numerous situations such as meetings, solving problems, negotiating agreements, answering emails, texts, and writing proposals. No matter what the activity, if we look at our day, we probably did not focus on one thing for a long period of time. If you want to become more creative and productive, you might want to reconsider how you divide your day with focus time for creative projects—the kinds of projects that inspire and energize us.

I personally divide my daily to-dos into three categories: *meaningful*, *mandatory*, and *mundane*. When I sort my activities this way, it helps me to keep focus on the to-dos that have more meaning. I always start my day with working on something meaningful, then I move to the mandatory, and if I get through those activities

I will work on the mundane. I encourage you to try this process. You will be pleased with the results it creates both mentally and emotionally.

When a new product is being birthed and developed, we can become mentally tired and stressed. The key is to maintain a balance in your life. Be aware of what is happening with your body. When you notice the stress creeping up on you, go take a walk, meditate, exercise, take a short vacation—do anything that will alleviate the stress and bring you back to hemostasis. If you allow chronic stress to dominate your body, it will take a toll on everything.

When I was developing Wanna-Be, I was moving at a very rapid pace. My days were filled with meetings, phone calls, working with designers, and manufactures in China. I was juggling lots of balls, and it took its toll on my family, marriage, health, finances, and just about everything in my life. To this day, I am not certain how I survived. Wanna-Be started out as a fun project, inspired by my soul's calling, and ended up being a daily emotional, physical, and mental drain. Additionally, keeping connected to my longing to express my spiritual and soul's calling had being dampened by the constant demands on my time. I was on 24-7 always thinking about the project, consumed by the constant and persistent pursuit to achieve my goal, never once taking the time to stop and give gratitude for what I was doing, and "why" I was doing it. I am convinced that when we get to this level of intense pursuit, we actually loose energy, focus, and concentration. We are off our game. Remember, balance in all areas of life is of utmost importance.

I didn't feel like I was connected with my soul at all. It was as if I had turned off the radio and was only hearing static signals and could not hear my soul's voice from within. I was so out of balance with every element of my life. As I reflect on this period, I still feel the emotional pain of a time where I had constructed everything backwards in my life. However, I will say that experiences like this one, where I was developing my first major product was an amazing learning experience, even though others would consider this a colossal failure.

I would not be the person I've become today had it not been for all the painful and challenging experiences of my past. I think that most of us can say that as well. The question I ask is: *Do you see your challenging and painful times as learning lessons or as painful experiences in your life?* The key to our personal growth is that we all take these lessons and grow personally, emotionally, mentally, and spiritually.

Here is a brief summary of some of my own challenging and painful times that I now see as learning lessons. I had a financial collapse that resulted in a Chapter 13 bankruptcy. I have been sued not once but several times. I have a son with Leukemia, who is thriving today as a result of miracle drugs. My younger son, who is an amazing young adult today, put my wife and myself through some very painful lessons because of his use of drugs, sex, and rock and roll. I have had business partnership breakups, a marriage that has almost failed several times, loss of a beautiful home that our family occupied for twenty-seven years to a short sale. My father died when I was eighteen years of age. I have lost friends who have died at very early ages, and recently there was the death of my mother who was the foundation and bedrock for our family. She was the "glue" that kept the peace and closeness in our immediate family.

No matter what the hardships in life they are gifted to us to help build our resilience. They serve a purpose to grow us emotionally and spiritually. We are certainly not here in the physical world to escape these difficult and challenging experiences. We are here to learn, grow, and make adjustments to how we perceive our world and the people that are blessing us through these enriched experiences.

Resistance is futile. The harder we resist our un-pleasurable life experiences, the slower we will learn from those experiences. Embrace the challenges, learn and grow forward knowing that these experiences don't need to be repeated—but occasionally they may. I've learned that the reason for re-living and repeating these unpleasant events is that our soul is speaking with us and is telling us that we are being prepared for much greater life experience.

Tapping into Your Positive Energy

Continuing to keep a positive mental attitude while going through challenging personal experiences requires resiliency, focus, determination, emotional strength and fortitude and knowing that the goal and dream you have is greater than the pain associated with reaching this goal. *We are never given more than we can handle or manage.*

Yet, during our challenges, it is easy to become very despondent and depressed. At times I felt like I wanted to commit hari-kari. (Japanese term for suicide). Yes, I have been depressed enough that the thought of suicide did enter my mind. In these deep dark personal times, I've learned that the only thing we can rely upon is our own close community of support, as well as the strength we receive from knowing that there is a power that exists that is greater than us and it wants us to succeed. My faith is in God; yours might be in another spiritual deity, but no matter what your knowings about spirituality, we do need an anchor that guides and lifts us up during our deepest, darkest hours.

So how did I personally tap into the energy to keep growing forward in spite of all my challenges? My spiritual practice which has transformed over the years has kept me focused on "knowing" the truth about who I really was—and that is a being of God. I was created in his likeness and my faith in a "higher power" has always rescued me from the crises that I created in my life.

Unequivocally, the energy comes from a connection with our soul. The voice inside that insists that we keep growing forward no matter what the circumstances. It encourages us when we are down; it loves us and nurtures us when we are depressed. Above all, we need to learn to listen to our soul's calling, and let it guide us through any and all challenges. It is always there for us if we just listen and tune into it. Our soul wants us to be happy, healthy, prosperous, and have joy in our lives.

Maya Angelou the great poet, speaker and writer was born to parents that she explains had a "calamitous marriage," and she was sent at a young age to live with her grandmother. She eventually moved back in with her mother, and at age eight was sexually assaulted by one of her mother's boyfriends. Add to that the racism she faced living in the Jim Crow South, and "overcoming adversity" begins to seem like an understatement.

Nevertheless, she did, being inspired by a teacher to read the works of Shakespeare, Poe and Dickens as well as stars of African-American literature as well. She drew upon this thirst for learning as well as the difficulties of her youth to produce some of the most dynamic and famous poems in twentieth century American literature.

Her poetry, including "I Know Why the Caged Bird Sings" earned Angelou everlasting fame and influence. President Bill Clinton recited one of her poems, "On the Pulse of the Morning," for his 1993 election, and President Barack Obama awarded her the highest civilian honor an American citizen can receive, the Presidential

Medal of Freedom, in 2011. By the time she passed away, Angelou had come to stand as one of the true American literary treasures.

There is overcoming adversity, and then there is overcoming racism and extreme personal horror. Mute for years after being sexually assaulted, she forever stands as an inspiration for anyone trying to find their voice after such trauma—and to speak and sing with as much poetic brilliance and beauty as the late, great Maya Angelou.

Angelou stands as an example of how powerful we truly are, when we choose to rise above adversity.

We are all a result of our own thinking. Think positive thoughts and we will have positive experiences manifesting in our lives. Think negative thoughts and we will attract negative experiences into our lives. It really is simple, and it is our choice.

We get to design our life how we wish, so why not make it joyous, happy and abundant.

It is a Mindset, not a Money Set

Many years ago I read a book by Dr. Jim Loehr and Tony Schwartz called *The Power of Full Engagement: Managing Energy, Not Time is the Key to High Performance and Personal Renewal*. The entire book was about how we use and manage our energy.

They stated,

> "Every one of our thoughts, emotions, and behaviors has an energy consequence for better or worse. The ultimate measure of our lives is not how much time we spend on this planet, but rather how much energy we invest in the time we have—performance, health, and happiness are grounded in the skillful management of energy."

Energy management and how to tap into that energy is the key to personal performance. It is everything in allowing us to sustain the required momentum on a project while keeping our professional and personal balance. Learn to manage your energy wisely and tap it to the optimum so you can sustain your forward growth and momentum in all that you have to do to obtain your dreams and goals.

Hacking the Gap of Personal Power

Personal power is based on strength, *confidence*, and competence that individuals gradually acquire over the course of their personal and professional development.

It is self-assertion, and a natural, healthy striving for love, satisfaction, and meaning in our interpersonal world. This type of power represents a movement toward self-realization and transcendent goals in life; its primary aim is mastery of self, not others.

Personal power is more an attitude or state of mind than an attempt to maneuver or control others. It is based on competence, vision, positive personal qualities, and service. When externalized, this power will be more generous, creative, and humane than other forms of power.

Hacking the Gap of our personal power provides access to that inner source (soul) that will propel us toward the successful completion of our ideas into the manifestation of our dreams.

Knowing What Jazzes You

We all have a happiness set point. In a recent interview with Nate Klemp, the author of *Start Here*, he stated, *"The set point is the unique spot that each of us occupies on the spectrum of life satisfaction: high, low, or somewhere in between."* He goes on to mention that there are three influencers of our set point: *judgment, attachment, and resistance.*

What an amazing realization. If you want to stay jazzed about something especially the birth of your product or service, then you need to remain joyous, happy, and engaged. If you can change your happiness set point by eliminating the judgments of yourself and others, imagine the impact this will have to your psyche. Judgment of the people and things in the world around us is a major cause for our unhappiness. When we judge, we are reflecting the inadequacies within ourselves. This behavior does not beget positive feelings about anyone, including ourselves.

Attachment to our expectation and the outcome of how we believe something should manifest in our lives, sets us up for disappointment if it does not turn out the way we envisioned. Have you ever written down a goal to acquire something, money, possessions, vacation etc. and the goal did not manifest as expected? Your vacation was not to Hawaii, but to see relatives in the Midwest. You were so attached to the idea that you were going to spend a week in Hawaii on the beach, that the trip to the Midwest to see your relatives was a real bummer.

Remember, it is your choice to keep a positive mindset about how it turns out and the impact that it has on your personal happiness. Attachments to expectations of how we believe things should turn out are the biggest disappointments we have in life. Those disappointments affect our personal happiness, which in turn affects your success.

Resistance is a personality trait and learned behavior that usually forms at a point in our life when we "didn't approve of our story." We did not like what was happing to us so we resisted the experience. You can certainly remember having seen children throw temper tantrums because they did not get what they wanted. Ultimately the parents give in because they cannot stand the crying and give the child what they want just to shut them up. As adults we do the same thing, it is a learned behavior and a natural one, I might add. This behavior of resistance arises from our fear and uncertainty. When there is an unknown event that happens to us, something that is unpredictable we can resist what is happening and create all kinds of negative thoughts and emotions. Ultimately, we don't really get what we want until we learn this lesson. And if we continue to resist, the results often lack the emotional and spiritual satisfaction we truly desire.

A great example of resistance was when my personal finances started to diminish. I could not keep up with the bills, credit cards, and mortgage payments. So I resisted the thought of filing for bankruptcy. I was not a quitter. I did not want to give up. That year of resistance, or avoidance, depleted our savings account just trying to keep up with the demands from the creditors. I did not want to admit that the best course of action would be to file for bankruptcy. In hindsight, the statement "pride goeth before the fall" was certainly ringing in my head.

Resistance to negative events in our life has a multiplying effect on our happiness. It usually is a slippery slope into despondency and depression. If one can only realize that the act of resistance itself is what causes our unhappiness. The sooner we realize this factor, and shift our behavior and beliefs, the sooner we can grow in our life, and choose for these experiences to be a stepping stone toward better times.

Your Personal Purpose and Values

I am eternally grateful for Kevin Mc Carthy, the author of a book entitled, *The On Purpose Person*, with a course of the same title. I was one of Kevin's biggest advocates and told as many people as I could about how taking his course changed my life forever. I not only defined my own powerful personal purpose statement as a result of taking his course, I developed a course called "*The Wayfinding Journey*," where I was teaching business owners about the power of personal purpose.

My values, mission, vision, and purpose were clarified as a result of Kevin's work. The act of putting into our consciousness our personal purpose, mission, vision and stating our values is the most powerful thing we can do. Our focus becomes clearer. We have a reason for doing what we are doing and we stop aimlessly drifting from one thing to another. As Kevin states, *"Your life is on purpose, not created by accident."*

This simple purpose statement changed my life: *"I exist to serve by inspiring passion."* I wanted to keep my purpose simple. It's meaning for me had to do with the interpretation of the word "passion."

In my purpose statement, the word passion is defined as, *a strong feeling or enthusiasm or excitement for somethi*ng. I thoroughly enjoy getting people excited about their initiatives, dreams, goals, projects, ideas, and inventions. I love fueling the fire of passion in their belly. It gives me great pleasure to help people find, sustain, and fuel the passion in their life, and to bring clarity where it previously it did not exist.

Finding your passion and honing on the work you love is important. Some of my personal values are: integrity, meaning, compassion, trust, engagement, empathy, serendipity, disruption, creativity, innovation, and playfulness.

What are some of your personal & professional values?

What do you stand for, and why do you stand for it?

Why do your values have such strong intrinsic meaning for you?

I encourage you to play with and explore your values; this will be the start of defining your personal purpose.

Once you have your values and purpose defined, it is like having a compass guiding you toward your North Star. You will experience new-found inspiration, energy and drive that will give you access to your soul. When your purpose and values are defined, it is as if a gateway to your inner soul is opened up and a flood of new energy flows in to your body and propels you toward your dreams.

Our Personal Vision

Developing a personal vision that very clearly resonates in our mind's eye is vital for our success. I realized for me, the practice of creating word pictures then having the ability to project them onto the screen of my mind as vivid pictures was a challenging exercise.

It was as if the vision was foggy and unclear, much like driving a car in a heavy fog where we cannot see where you are going. Nobody likes to drive in heavy fog; we all like to have a clear picture of the terrain and our surrounds.

So what is the secret to accessing these vivid pictures and being able to keep them in the forefront of your minds eye? First, it is practice, patience, and thoughtful development of the pictures of your future vision. This comes from accessing your soul, listening to the voice, and drawing the pictures of your future life. Trust in what you are being guided to do—really trust the voice of your intuition. There are many tools that have been developed to aid us in the process. I personally like using mind mapping software. There are several of them that I have used over the years, including *iMindMap9* and *Mind Meister*. I also have adopted the use of a cloud-based program called *Goalscape*. Goalscape is especially helpful in working on personal goals as well as with teams to collaborate your joint efforts toward the successful completion of your group goals.

It might seem like craziness, but if you will trust in the process, you will see that it is all for your greater good. The soul is there to guide, direct, and help you manifest the best self you can be. Your personal vision plays an important role in guiding, inspiring, and giving you clarity of direction. It is the blueprint to a meaningful and more fulfilling life.

The Soul of Goals—Building a Blueprint for Better Living

A goal without soul is more like a to-do list than a goal. I personally have written goals for years, and when I first started, I found that they were flat and meaningless. The goals did not have the energy that was required to keep my attention and focus to see them to completion. The goals were more ideas that I "thought" would be good for me. I definitely didn't have the "buy-in," nor did they resonate with my values or purpose. So the process of checking the boxes when they were completed was arduous, boring, and lifeless.

A soulful goal when emanating from your higher self has significant positive energy. We can feel it in our body. We are excited to be focused on it. It wakes us up in the morning; it keeps us up at night, and it fuels an internal flame that cannot be extinguished. With a desire, drive, and passion to accomplish a goal, because it has significant meaning and is aligned with our values and purpose—we will experience success.

A goal with soul ignites us and propels us forward; it removes inertia and drives the development of a new product or service. We really want to manifest our creative ideas into reality. We can visualize and feel what it is like to have people using our service or product. It brings us tremendous joy and personal gratification knowing that we have succeeded.

Goals with soul are never driven by money or the attainment of great monetary success; however, monetary success is an outcome of doing the right thing. When we are personally driven by our soul telling us what to do, we remain inspired, and feel a sacred duty to complete what we are working on—no matter what the consequences. We know it is right, no matter what others might tell us.

Without soul, goals are flat and energy less. It's like going through the motions when our goals do not have meaning and significance. Most of the time goals without soul are *not* achieved, and if they are, we are not excited by their achievement.

DON'T ALLOW MUNDANE DISTRACTIONS TO REMOVE YOU FROM APPLYING YOUR TALENTS TO YOUR WILDLY IMPORTANT GOALS.

When establishing goals with soul you need to dig deep inside, find what will keep you ignited, inspired, and will sustain the momentum of your soul's desire. When you listen to your soul, it keeps the vision present in your mind's eye and ultimately your idea will come to fruition.

Stay focused; call in your soul, by spending time in silence and meditation, and listen to that gentle voice within that frequently can be drowned out by sensual desires of life.

Your blueprint for better living is the outcome of being focused on working from a position of your higher purpose. You are to stay committed to something of significance that will impact your life and the lives of thousands of others. Your blueprint once completed is not only duplicable, but is part of your personal DNA. You can reach for even higher and loftier goals next time. With each new idea or goal, you can go further and more significant results will manifest from focused application of your energies.

Once you've completed this inspiring process, you will feel accomplished. When you have a breakthrough like this, you will never return to the old you, the person that was going through the motions wondering if there was more to life.

The singer Peggy Lee used to sing a song called "Is That All There Is" and believe me there is more; there is significance, meaning, and wonder in life and you were given an opportunity to experience this wonder. So don't allow resistance to side track you, don't allow your ego to guide you off track, and don't allow others to dissuade you to go back to your life of *going through the motions*.

This world needs more inventors and ideas that will disrupt and ignite the desire in others to awaken human potential in all. We need you to transform the consciousness of society and of our world, and create a new mindset that uplifts souls everywhere to see that there is more to life than going through the motions. Let's spark within all souls walking on the planet a desire to learn and explore new way of being and doing, with the desire to help our civilization thrive in these very exciting times.

Hacking the Gap of the blueprint for better living requires that we all awaken to our unlimited possibilities. At this point you might be saying that "Greg, you are too optimistic," or "You have done too many podcasts with personal growth authors," and that would be a fact. This is a big reason for my personal optimism, and one of the reasons for wanting to encourage you to look for the best in yourself.

It is too damn easy to get down on ourselves. Believe me, I have been there and it is a real bummer. Once the cycle starts, then depression set in and if the downer mentality continues, the outcome can require psychological intervention or medication. I am happy to report that I have never been on Zoloft or any anti-depressant medications, but I certainly have been clinical depressed.

If you are interested in learning more about how to treat depression without medications, here is a great book on how to get yourself out of depression, is by Dr. James Gordon, entitled *Unstuck—Your Guide to the Seven Stage Journey Out of Depression.* Dr. Gordon approaches depression from a mind-body approach and provides the reader with techniques to move them out of depression without medications.

It is very easy to become non-compliant and not want to take the prescription or follow the advice, and where does that lead?

It leads us in an insidious cycle of doing the same thing and expecting a different result—that is Albert Einstein's definition of insanity.

Mindset Applications for Hacking the Gap for Better Living

The following are my prescriptions for *Hacking the Gap* for a better life. Remember the key to any prescription is to follow the advice.

- Set intentions and give gratitude upon waking up in the morning.

- Remove judgment for others and self-judgment from your thinking. This requires work and reminding yourself that you are in the process—and judgment is highly detrimental to a better life.

- Set goals with soul and don't fill up your day with a list of to-dos without meaning and that are not aligned with your values and purpose.

- Try the technique of dividing your goals into three categories: meaningful, mandatory and mundane. Work first thing in the morning on meaningful goals and you will find that your daily focus changes for the good.

- Take the time to define your values and purpose in life, and learn to live by them.

- Give back; find something that you are passionate about—a cause, charity or personal passion; give the gift of time, money or in whatever way possible.

- Develop a mastermind group, or meet with associates or like-minded friends. The goal here is to be supported and challenged at the same time. This is a definite must if you want to grow and have a more meaningful life.

- Read something positive daily—a book, blog, article, or quotes. If you are trying to stimulate your creativity and connect new neuro-pathways. The science recommends reading something that is opposite of what you normally read. So if you read personal growth books all the time, try reading a novel.

- Stay away from the negative news. We are bombarded with immediate news from our cell phones, TV, Internet, iPads, and this can be a real downer. If you need to know do it quickly and only once per day.

- Write positive affirmation(s) or mantra and keep them in front of your computer or on a 3x5 cards and carry them with you throughout the day.

- Give yourself breaks from your work. Take a walk, commune with nature, exercise. Whatever you do, take a pause. It has been proven that we reach a point of satiation and our minds need a break from the computer or whatever we are working on.

If you want more *Hacking the Gap* ideas please go to www.hackingthegap.com where I have a list of over fifty ideas that you can implement into your life to create the best blueprint for better living.

INNOVATION
Creating & Building

CHAPTER 7

INNOVATION:
Creating, Designing and Building Your Products, Services and Reinventing Yourself in the Process

"Failure is an option here. If things are not failing, you are not innovating enough."
—Elon Musk

The journey to innovating a product or service can and usually does start with a process of reinventing ourselves. When we develop something new, we are entering a personal rebirthing process. This starts by making a connection to our intuition and soul then listening to the voice for guidance and direction. We are learning new skills and exploring frontiers where we have never been before. This journey is filled with all kinds of emotions such as excitement, joy, apprehension, uncertainty, fear, and doubt. Change is one of the most uncomfortable processes we grow through, and when we look back at the journey, we are often grateful because we have become a better person for the experience.

When we are in the innovation stage, we are working on something new everyday. These experiences and events can range from meeting with designers to developing a prototype or sourcing a supplier for a resource that is required to go into the new product. No matter what the action, if this is new to us, we are exploring new frontiers—places, people, and processes that will bring up both excitement and some degree of fear and doubt about our abilities. This is because we have never been in this position before, it's uncharted territory.

Innovating and inventing a new product and growing our ideas are exciting, not only because it's new, but because it is an expression of our soul's desire—and requires expansion of our world.

"BE ON THE LOOKOUT FOR SURPRISES WHEN INVENTING SOMETHING NEW. IT'S LIKE UNEXPLORED TERRITORY AND YOU NEVER KNOW WHAT UNCHARTED TERRAIN YOU WILL HAVE TO NAVIGATE."

I like to use the analogy of planning a vacation to someplace new, and not knowing what to expect, or planning a hiking trip into the wilderness. There are lots of unknowns, but there is an exhilaration associated with the adventure because we are exploring new frontiers. We might have a map or use our GPS, but we still don't know what the terrain or path is going to be like. These experiences allow our adventurous self to be expressed, and the creative side of our brains to go to work. We are solving problems at rapid speed, and making new connections of the synapses of our brain, resulting in a well thought out plan for our trip.

Just as we prepare for a trip, we prepare to develop a product, idea, or service. While there are unknowns and uncertainties about how something might work or fit together, we have a knowing, a sense of certainty about the end product, and we're committed to manifesting our idea into reality.

> Innovation by its definition is a "new idea, device or method." Innovation is "often also viewed as the application of better solutions that meet new requirements, unarticulated needs, or existing market needs." So by its definition we are examining, testing, and innovating something new—a product or service that will make the old product or service obsolete.
> —Wikipedia, S. Maryville (1992)

In a recent interview with Heather McGowan, the co-author of *Disrupt Together How Teams Consistently Innovates*, she stated that many of the new inventions are improvements on existing technology or services.

Below is a list of just some of the technologies that have been replaced or improved with newly designed products in the last twenty years:

- The Palm Pilot (PDA) replaced by Smartphones.

- Paid email accounts you have to pay for, replaced by free Gmail
- Dial Up and Pay Phones, replaced by Smartphones
- Getting film developed, replaced by digital pictures
- Movie rental stores, replaced by Netflix
- Thomas Brothers (Maps), replaced by GPS device on our smartphones.
- Phone landlines, replaced by Skype, VOIP etc.
- Long Distance Charges, replaced by VOIP etc.
- VCR, replaced by DVR
- Fax machines, replaced by scanners and PDFs being sent with email.
- Phone books, dictionaries and encyclopedias, replaced by the Internet
- Calling 411 for information, replaced by Smartphone search
- CDs replaced by digital download to Smartphone or iPods.

All of these inventions came about as a result of someone thinking of a more effective way of achieving an improved result. Because of the efficiency, the general public was willing to adopt the new technology to help save time and money in the long run.

Keep in mind that many of the new technologies were not initially inexpensive. As a matter of fact, the investment might have been more than the current technology we were utilizing, but because we saw the benefits, we were willing to make the change and adopt the new technology to hopefully improve our lives.

Setting the Stage to Innovate

Tapping into our soul and finding new ways to innovate requires that you observe, listen and ask questions about how a current product or services is being utilized. Frequently, ideas are disruptive to the current technology, and that is a good thing. Some recent examples of disruption to services to hotels and taxis would be *Airbnb, Uber,* and *Lift.*

Disruptions to technology are continuously happening. Wearable devices to monitor our pulse, calorie expenditure and steps, and wireless connectivity in creating a smart home, regulating thermostats, lights, and other electronic devices remotely are some examples. We even have cars that drive themselves.

Our role as investigators and sleuths is to focus our attention on what can be improved and made better. Our hunches come from our intuition, which leads to insights, then a recording of the ideas. Once we've landed on the idea, done our homework, and experienced the realization that our idea is new, and never been developed the way we envision it, we become inspired. Where our ideas meet inspiration is a magical point, for this inspiration is being fueled by our soul. We know we are on to something big when it is hard to let up.

Have you ever watched *Shark Tank* the show where hundreds of hopeful entrepreneurs come on the TV show to get a "deal" with the sharks? I have been a fan of that show for years and have seen some really great new ideas develop into viable products and/or services. The main component of a successful product or services is always "the better mouse trap," the "disruptive" factor that excited the shark tank into a frenzy.

I recently was watching an episode and an inventor brought on a new product called "Biem." This device allowed you to melt a stick of butter into a liquid so that it could be sprayed out of the device. Both my wife and I thought this was a great idea. We would definitely use a product like this for cooking and to butter popcorn. This is an example of a better mouse trap. There have been hundreds of products that over the years of that show have been turned into amazing successes and generated millions of dollars in sales for the inventors and their companies. If they can do it, so can you.

What makes your product different and unique is your ability and willingness to make mistakes, and believe me you will make lots of mistakes. In this iterative process whether you are designing the product or service by yourself or with a team of people you need to be open to working and reworking your idea. Consider all ideas and suggestions from your team or others who are providing you with advice, then test and retest. The incubation stage is vitally important to the evolution of your product, idea or service. Don't attempt to force things; anything that is unnatural and forced is not going to improve your design.

Playing and having fun is a key element to the development of anything new. Play sparks innovative ideas, and fosters enjoyment in the process, so remember to play and enjoy your journey. Designing and developing something new is both play and hard work. You will hit mental barriers and roadblocks. Your patience will be tested multiple times over. Be patient with yourself and the others on your team. Be open to exploring, breaking, testing and rebuilding your product or service. Keep a perspective that you are working on a long-term project. Your new product or service is likely to have a long run before it becomes obsolete or someone invents something better—if you make it the best it can be through this process.

Business Innovation— Differentiating Your Business or Service from the Crowd

Much has been written about the red ocean, blue ocean theory. A red ocean is where your product or service is considered a commodity, and you are competing in a well-developed market.

A good example of this would be the soft drink industry. The Big corporate players—Coke and Pepsi—dominate this industry, and lots of other start-ups over the last fifty years that have not been able to succeed in such a competitive market. We see hundreds of new soft drinks come on the market annually, and some succeed and others fail.

A new revolution in the market that just peaked $157 million in sales, but would be considered a blue ocean market, is what is termed a relaxation beverage industry. Such products as Just Chill, Marley Beverage Company, and Dream Water, touted as sleep, work, and study aids, are products that will differentiate themselves in an amazingly competitive sea of red ocean soft drink products.

So with this understanding of the concept of red and blue ocean, what are you doing to differentiate yourself in an area where there is already competition?

What is your unique differentiator?

What makes you unique from the crowd?

What problem are you solving for your consumer?

Who are you solving that problem for?

While these questions are easy to ask, they are not always easy to answer. Without sounding like a broken record, one of the only ways to differentiate yourself is to ask questions from deep within and listen to your soul's answers. Once you have tapped into this amazing resource, you will be guided and given advice on what will make your product and service outstanding and different. Insights about what to do or what direction to take frequently come from symbols and signs, and not just voices from you inner soul. You will see a symbol or a sign that crosses your path or flashes in your mind's eye. That symbol or sign is attempting to provide you with guidance.

WHAT PROBLEM ARE YOU SOLVING FOR YOUR CUSTOMERS?

My personal experience with this has been the recurring sign of 11:11 or 1:11 on a clock, or cell phone, oven timer and car clock. I constantly am receiving this sign. So just what does it mean?

According the astrologists and psychics, this means that I am in synchronicity with the pulse of life, that I am open and aware to my intuition and in alignment with its desire to provide me with new insights, ideas, and openness to being creative. These synchronicities provide me with the reassurance that whatever I'm working on is in alignment with my soul's calling.

So no matter what signs you might be receiving, become aware of the messages being sent to you by the universe. Be open that you are being guided and observe what is happening to you and around you.

Robert Moss the author of a wonderful book entitled *Sidewalk Oracles-Playing with Signs, Symbols, and Synchronicity in Everyday Life*, has interviewed hundreds about their experience with signs, symbols, and oracles. The recounts of these stories and the meaningful connections that occurred as a result of paying attention to the signs and symbols are truly wonderful.

An example of how this works is very simple. Robert was speaking with me on the podcast about the fact that he was concerned that he had taken on two projects at once, and that he might not be able to do justice to both of the projects.

He was out walking his Schnauzer, and he passed a contractor that said in jest, *"Your dog certainly could not kill both of us at once."* This obviously had significant meaning for him, because he was considering dividing his time between the two projects. So he proceeded to call the person that he had committed to doing the second project with and explained that he didn't believe he could do it justice. The response from the person was for him to reconnect when he had the time to dedicate his skills to the project. When we are in tune to these signs and symbols, we can use the messages to our benefit. Just be aware and open to listening, seeing, and sensing what is happening in the environments around you.

Distractions, Attachment, Resistance— the Killers of Innovation and Personal Growth

Distractions are everywhere. They keep us from our focus and will divert the energy that is required to complete our goal and reach our dream.

In a recent interview with Adam Gazzaley, the co-author of *The Distracted Mind: Ancient Brains in a High Tech World*, he stated:

> "We have come to believe that the human brain is a master navigator of the river of information that rages steadily all around us. And yet we often feel challenged when trying to fulfill even fairly simple goals. This is the result of interferences—both distractions from irrelevant information and interruptions by our attempts to simultaneously pursue multiple goals. Many of you may now be glancing accusingly at your mobile phone. But before we place any blame on this potential culprit, it is critical to understand that our sensitivity to interference, or what we will refer to throughout this book as 'the Distracted Mind' was not born out of modern technology. But rather, it is a fundamental vulnerability of our brains."

Emotional distractions that emanate from our mind might come from negative self-judgment. This will raise its ugly head at some point in our product development lifecycle. To keep emotional distractions from derailing our progress, we need to recognize it and be aware that it is happening and nip it in the bud. It only has one purpose and that is to insert self-doubt, fear, and uncertainty about the development of our ideas. It is the number one enemy to getting projects completed.

The way to subvert these thoughts from entering our mind would be to find a space where we can connect from within. This means to mindfully schedule breaks during the day that allow us to detach from the chaos of our busy lives, and ask, "What's next? What's getting in my way?" Listen deeply and attempt to find the proper signal of your soul. One that is positive and reassuring. When we hear the negative, we are tuned into the wrong frequency, and we are on the channel of negativity.

Thomas Edison once said,

"Our greatest weakness lies in giving up. The most certain way to succeed is always to just try one more time."

"MANY OF LIFE'S FAILURES ARE PEOPLE WHO DID NOT REALIZE HOW CLOSE THEY WERE TO SUCCESS WHEN THEY GAVE UP."

Ignoring these thoughts and drowning them out can only be completed by your willingness to open up to your superconscious mind. Our superconscious mind where it connects us to our soul, inspiring us to re-focus on our dreams and providing us with solutions on how to manifest our dreams into reality.

Other forms of distraction are developed by creating improper boundaries—with our technology, with our team, with our family and more. We need to diligently protect our time from infringements by individuals who have their own agenda to follow. We also need to address our lack of discipline to stay away from emails, social media, and the news. There is nothing wrong with unplugging and putting a sign on the door—virtual or otherwise—that we're not to be disturbed so that we can do what we're being called to do—*create*!

Attachments can derail our plans as well. We all can become attached to our ideas; we often behave like a dog with a bone. We sink our teeth into the idea and just don't want to give up on it. Attachments to an idea or outcome can be very dangerous, stifling creativity and new possibilities of which we are not aware.

You might be saying to yourself that I am contradicting myself—well let me explain. It is great to have conviction, commitment, and persistence in getting something done, to manifesting an idea but not by being rigid. Pliability allows us to remain in the flow of life. It opens us up to alternative solutions and ways of solving the problem. Being too rigid and set on the idea that the expected result has to go exactly as we planned is not good. The creative process requires that we be flexible and open to the possibilities that we often don't see until they are upon us. Trust and openness are key to pliability.

It's ironic but as I am writing this chapter in the book I am in a co-work office, and in the office next door I can hear a song by the Rolling Stones playing: *"You can't always get what you want, but if you try something you find, you get what you need."* How true that is. Try something you find and you will get what you need. It might not be exactly what you expect. It's likely to be much better.

Keep an open mind, stay in the flow of life, and allow insight from your intuition and feedback from others to influence how your idea might take form.

If you speak with software engineers, the creative and innovative process is usually completed with small teams of people and their combined cooperation is imperative. Personalities and egos need to be checked at the door. Cooperation, sharing, and open-mindedness are a key component to the evolution of an idea. What is being created is a culmination of the collective consciousness and experience from the subconscious of all the people involved. You were guided to birth this new idea, but the ultimate completion of that idea and the development into a viable software product will be a joint effort. Being playful, pliable and open to collaborative thought is a critical element to the success, evolution, and birth of your new idea.

Resistance is different from your attachment to the outcome of your thoughts being manifested into your product or service. Personal resistance is a killer of all innovation. Resistance can rear its ugly head during any phase of a project—which is why I've repeated my caution about resistance throughout the book. Resistance can prevent us from initiating action on an idea or modifying an idea based on feedback. Either way, resistance blocks the flow of creativity.

Let's use the example of electrical flow to illustrate the point:

> **Electrical resistance of a conductor is the measure of the difficulty to pass electric current through that conductor. The inverse of resistance is electrical conductance, and this is the ease at which an electrical current passes.**

We want to allow the flow of ideas, and this only happens when we are a conductor of that electrical flow.

Our body is filled with electricity. Our heart beat is created by an electrical impulse that beats approximately 4,800 times per hour, 115, 200 times per day, over the course of a year 42,048,000—and in a lifetime 3,368,840,000 times.

How often do we even give this miracle a thought? Probably not too often, unless you are dealing with heart issues or have had heart disease. Yet, this is an example of natural flow, just like the flow you want to occur with your project. Personal resistance blocks the flow of currents or ideas. Keep an open mind, heart, and reception to everything around you, observe and be aware. Look for signs that guide you. There are messages just waiting to inform you about the evolution of your ideas. Remain open, receptive, and a conductor of the magic of your own electrical current and flow.

Paying Attention— A Window to the World

Having the proper environment to incubate ideas is necessary to the successful completion and development of any product, service, or idea. We do this by making our surrounds optimal for our performance, thereby creating the environment that is conducive to tapping into the deepest levels of our consciousness—and assisting us in *Hacking the Gap*.

Remember the definition of *Hacking the Gap is the shortest distance between two points with the least amount of resistance while growing personally and reaching our highest human potential.* This requires that we pay attention, remain focused, and align all of our surroundings to allow for this convergence of energy. In the

Hacking the Gap process, we must be in the zone or flow. When this occurs, we are not blocked by anything and time stands still. Yet often what blocks us are the distractions we allow into our environment—messy desks, dishes in the sink, relationship issues, and much more.

When the window to our world is clear of any obstacles, we have laser focus for the refinement of ideas that maturate, expand, and enliven the original idea. During our creative process when we are open to receiving a new perspective, the world expands and morphs into something that allows us to see and experience insights into solving problems. We gain a heightened intuitive sense about what will improve our inventions or idea, or what needs to be left behind because it no longer supports the development of our ideas.

When we are working in a collective consciousness with several designers, or developers, hopefully all of the team sees their world with a broader perspective. Convergence and synchronicity occurs and the team has breakthroughs that lead to the product being improved. From the example above, the electrical current is open and flowing allowing for the convergence and synchronicity of ideas to merge into a collective breakthrough.

Inevitably, we will experience periods of blockage, breakdown, and rebuilding, but by paying attention and having an open mind, we can view the window to the world, allowing new perspectives to broaden our viewpoints, leading to synchronicity and serendipity.

If we are committed to continually learning by reading and study-ing with a veracious appetite to apply our new found knowledge, it is inevitable that we will develop ideas that can be formulated into new products or services. In our world today with the speed of transformation and adoption of technology, it requires that we adopt, adapt, and be willing to transform through a willingness to learn new ways. This is how we personally grow when bringing a new idea into fruition. It is impossible not to have a personal transformative experience as a result of the birth and evolution of an idea.

Focus on the Journey, Not the Destination

In the book *Deep Work, Rules for Focused Success in a Distracted World*, Cal Newport cites a story about Jerry Seinfeld. A budding comedian asked Seinfeld how to become a better comedian. Seinfeld replied that he needed to write a new joke every day and that he should keep a calendar on his wall and put a red "X" on each day that he wrote a new joke. Seinfeld said, *"After a few days you'll have a chain. Just keep doing it and the chain will grow longer every day. You'll like seeing that chain, especially when you get a few weeks under your belt. Your only job next is to not break the chain."* This *chain method* (as some now call it) soon became a hit among writers and fitness enthusiasts—communities that thrive on the ability to do hard things consistently.

It takes lots of hard work, persistence, and willingness to sacrifice to see any innovation come to life. Hard work and dedication do pay off. Intrinsically when we are on purpose and doing something that has high value and meaning you are bound to be naturally creative and inventive. Unfortunately, many will never get to experience this wonderful and fulfilling life experience because they are not paying attention to the details in their lives—and creating chains of experience.

Employee engagement is at an all time low with over 71% of all employees not fully engaged in their work. That means that only 29% of employee are engaged and enjoying the work they do.

Yet it's important to point out that companies with fully engaged employees outperform their competitors by 202%.

So when we focus on the destination of *"getting off work"* or *"taking our next vacation,"* this is an indication that we're lacking purpose and meaning in our life. And if this is you, it could mean that the idea for the product or service you are pursuing might not be a good idea... and not an innovation sparked by your personal passion and purpose.

Our journey here on the planet is about doing the work we're called to do—learning, growing, while having experiences that some may deem as "good" or others not so good. And this must come from our inner knowing, an inner spark, not just a good idea cooked up on a whim. When we commit to what we're called to do, we grow, transform, and open up to new possibilities. We have to be willing to risk, broaden our perspective, and see our world with new eyes. We need to question if we are happy with a current situation. If not, we need to determine what makes us happy, fulfilled, and have a zest for life.

If what we're doing doesn't bring happiness and joy into our lives, then we need to take the time to reflect, talk with friends, family and associates to see what they might be doing that inspires them or at least get a fresh perspective about what they might be doing that brings them joy. Read personal growth books, listen to podcasts, and go on retreats for some inspiration. The library of resources to inspire us, and provide our minds with positive personal growth is incredible, if we'll only take the time to access it.

Many of us journey through life without a roadmap—directionless without aim, purpose, and a cause. It does not have to be this way. Life is meant to be lived on purpose. We need to do the things that need to be part of our daily routine as like the example of marking an "X" on the calendar. When we do the little things, we are on the way to accomplishing the big things.

Malcolm Gladwell in his book *Outliers* said, "Practice isn't the thing you do once you're good. It's the thing you do that makes you good." *He contends that the magic 10,000 hours' rule of the application and practice of our skills is what sets us apart from others and a definite key to our success.*

So we need to remember that hopefully our life will be a long and enriched journey, and our focus needs to remain on the little things that we do daily to become better at our skill, whether that be writing, art, music, woodworking, yoga, or creating jokes…When we do this, our personal rewards will be happiness, fulfillment, joy, and meaning in our life.

Eliminating Time Constraints, Stress, and Anxiety

I spent years running my life by the clock, always late for another appointment or meeting. I had clocks everywhere reminding me of what had to be done knowing that I probably would not get it completed in the time remaining. It took me fifty-five years before I was aware of what I was doing to myself by running my life by the clock.

We all know that time is something that is manmade. Previous generations of people including settlers, Indians and explores used sundials and the change of season to measure the passing of time.

This completely new perspective has sped up our internal biological clocks, and we now are more aware of time than any of our previous generations. Everywhere there are cell phones, car clocks, or computer displays reminding us of the passing of time—not by seasons but by seconds, minutes, days, weeks, and months. This consistent reminder about time creates stress and anxiety, if we allow it to become an integral part of our life. To slow down and enjoy life, to remove the time constraints, stress, and anxiety requires that we plan our day and our life. We all have so much we can do, but we need to question if it is really necessary and part of the pursuit of our purpose and life meaning.

In the book, *Essentialism: The Disciplined Pursuit of Less*, author Greg McKeown states that,

> "The way of the essentialist means living by design, not by default. Instead of making choices reactively, the Essentialist deliberately distinguishes the vital few from the trivial many, eliminates the nonessentials, and then removes obstacles so the essential things have clear, smooth passage. In other words, Essentialism is the disciplined, systematic approach for determining where our highest point of contribution lies, then making execution of those things almost effortless."

If we could all live our lives as, Essentialists instead of Non-Essentialists, we all would be happier. I know from personal experience by living my life from always needing more, not being enough and surrounding myself with physical things, gadgets, cars, and toys thinking that it would make me happy, I not only was less happy, I was a stressed out mess. I had the attention span of a gnat, chasing from one shiny object to another thinking that something would bring me more happiness, and those shiny object only brought on more stress and obligation to pay for all the stuff I was acquiring. I was spending money I didn't have, on things that I didn't need, with the ultimate result throwing me into personal bankruptcy.

My personal stress was so intense that it almost killed me. I was a physical wreck, with anxiety attacks, heart palpitations, and numerous visits to the cardiologist. I spent over a year in bio-feedback reconditioning my behaviors to help eliminate some of the stress. The biofeedback practices lead me to adopting a new practice of meditation, mindfulness, and a spiritual pursuit—to take a deep look inside at my beliefs and conditioning. These new adopted practices of meditation and finding a meaningful spiritual path were what saved my life—and opened me up to consider what was essential in my life.

Time constraints, stress, and anxiety lead you down a path of distraction, and will kill your intuition, ideas, and innovation. If you want to be optimally innovative, in the flow and alive with new ideas, then focusing on activities that create stress and anxiety needs to be avoided at all costs. Remove anything that could distract you or take you off track. Eliminate as many of the stresses as you possibly can from your life and learn to focus. Practice and make your craft perfect. The perfection of your craft will keep you focused on your purpose, and when you are focused on your purpose, you will be able to sustain the energy and inspiration required to develop, design, test, and incubate your ideas.

Mindset Applications for Hacking the Gap of Innovation

If you want to *Hack the Gap* toward better innovations, I have some simple mindset applications that you can make part of your life, and hopefully this will make things easier for you.

If you practice these applications as part of your habits and routines you will find that it is making the process of stepping into innovating easier and more fun.

- Innovating a new product is hard work. Don't forget to do the little things and put "X" on your calendar to remind yourself of your win along the way.

- Self-judgment is your nemesis; remind yourself that you are on purpose. Read your purpose statement and affirmations daily. Create a mantra for those times you begin to doubt yourself. *I can do anything one day at a time.*

- Do not get attached to the outcome of what you believe is the "right" way. There are many paths up the mountain, and they all lead to the same destination.

- Resistance is futile. Stay in the flow of life by being open. Collaborate with others. Ask for advice and take it all in but only be influenced by what serves you and moves the projects forward.

- Broaden your perspective and open up to the window to the world. Read, listen, observe, and look for signposts. The more you can do this the quicker your idea will be manifest into reality.

- You are on a journey both personally and professionally. Your personal and spiritual growth is happening as a result of your willingness to take on this project. Enjoy the journey—journal your experience and read what you have written. Your entries will amaze you.

- Become an Essentialist in the process of your journey. Remove all the unnecessary distractions and focus your attention on the one single thing—the development of your product or service. A good daily practice would be to write out the essential and necessary things to accomplish, not the mundane and meaningless. Focus, concentrate, and apply your critical thinking skills.

- Eliminate time constraints that cause you stress. While you might not have an unlimited budget to bring your product or service to market, stressing yourself out over time will only make it worse—and you will make more mistakes. Remove clocks, cell phones, and any reference to time when you sit down to work on your project. You will find that "time" flies.

- Start your day with quiet time, reflection, or meditation. Give yourself at least fifteen minutes. After you have done this practice, write down the immediate thoughts or ideas that come into your mind after your meditation. Scan those ideas to see if they have any relevance to your core idea, and the development of your product or service.

IMPLEMENTATION
Growing Your Business

CHAPTER 8

IMPLEMENTATION:
Growing Your Business with Actions and Accountability

"Having authority implies accountability. If you reject the blame for failures under your watch, people reject your leadership."
—Rick Warren, founder and senior Pastor of the Saddleback Church, author of *The Purpose Driven Life*

The implementation stage is an exciting time for anyone developing a new idea, product, or service. As we move through the stages of development, implementation is the point at which you are ready for the launch. This stage is filled with its own challenges, because there are many factors to consider. Yet, the excitement of getting our product launched far exceeds any apprehension we might have.

We get to execute our marketing and sales plans. We get to see if the public is open, ready, and willing to purchase our amazing new products. We have the distinct opportunity to field customer complaints and experience demands on our resources for more marketing dollars. And for this you must develop a good sales team. You will be asked for better collateral, changes to the sales agreements, and website improvements—and a good team is worth every penny of investment.

As the visionary for your product, you need to remain vigilant and aware of how you are utilizing your time. At this stage in the product development, you can easily become distracted and lose focus. However, now is the time to stay engaged. I received some great advice on how to do just that from author Josh Davis in, *Two Awesome Hours—Science-Based Strategies to Harness Your Best Time and Get Your Most Important Work Done.* He states that to stay focused we need to master two skills:

> "The first is obvious—to remove distractions—and learning more about how attention works can help motivate us to take that seriously enough. The second is paradoxical. Of all the strategies for being highly productive I offer in this book, this one is perhaps the most confounding. We have to let our minds wander. That's right. Let that tight grip on attention go. In short our attention systems seem to have been built for scanning and detection. Thus, it is wholly unnatural to focus without wandering. If you have failed at maintaining continual focus throughout your work sessions, rejoice. If you had, you'd be remarkably dysfunctional."

However, some entrepreneurs wander too far. They fall into complacency and lose sight of what needs to be accomplished during the implementation stage. The complacency occurs because the original creative energy that helped to get the idea developed to this point is not perceived to be as important as it was during the ideation stage. It is completely normal to spend less of your time on all the logistics of delivery, marketing, sales, etc., but only if you have transferred ownership of the project to a trusted and competent leader on your team to manage the implementation phase. If you are a small organization, I would caution against releasing the reigns. Our creative input is especially important at this point of the product launch.

However, you have permission to divest yourself of some of your energy, but not to disappear from sight. I've seen too many companies where the founder/visionary removes him or herself from the operations, and operations start to become chaotic and disorganized. When the energy of the inventor or entrepreneur becomes fragmented, complex issues start to arise, such as accountability, leadership, and financial risk.

Employees, partners, and or investors can soon become disappointed when the visionary becomes inaccessible and his or her interests wane during this implementation stage. The leadership team still needs the guidance and counsel of the founding visionary to propel the project to successful execution. Yet some time away from the intensity of the launch is called for if we want to keep our creative juices flowing.

In his recent book *Deep Work* author Cal Newport writes about having a bimodal philosophy of deep work verses that of a monastic philosophy of deep work. He says that,

> **"The bimodal philosophy belief is that deep work can produce extreme productivity, but only if the subject dedicates enough time to such endeavors to reach maximum cognitive intensity—the state in which real breakthroughs occur."**

He recommends that the minimum unit of time should be at *least one full day.* To put aside a few hours in the morning, for example, is too short to count as a deep work stretch for an adherent of this approach. It is our responsibility as visionaries to stay focused, to pay attention, and be aware of what is transpiring around the launch of our product or service.

This *one full day* dedicated to deep work is to be without distractions, phone calls, or interruptions. Lock yourself away, be a recluse, and let people know that this is your time to keep working on and refining the idea, product, or service.

The Habits, Behavior, and Patterns that Affect our Productivity

We all live in a world where the tantalizing and shiny objects titillate us to move off course at almost any time. So congratulate yourself on getting to the implementation stage. You have successfully thwarted off thousands of distractions that could have diverted your energy and even discouraged you enough to abandon your vision. You have been successful, and believe me, most people are not successful at getting to the implementation stage. You have delayed gratification. You put in the extra effort and long hours that allow you to see the manifestation of your vision.

When you move into the implementation stage—the *how* you do something is as equally important as the *what* to do in accomplishing your goal. As they say in the Nike commercials, "Just Do It."

The studies of Clayton Christensen, a Harvard Business School professor, explored *The 4 Discipline of Execution* that later became a best-selling book that was written by authors Chris McChesney, Sean Covey, and Jim Huling.

They describe the four disciplines of execution (4DX) as:

1. **Focus on the Wildly Important.** They elaborate that execution should be aimed at a small number of "wildly" important goals. This simplicity will help focus an organization's energy.

2. **Act on Lead Measures.** "There are two types of measures: lag measures and lead measures. Lag measures describe the things you're ultimately trying to improve. Lead measures on the other hand, measure the new behaviors that will drive success on lag measure." In other words, lead measures turn your attention to improving the behaviors you directly control in the near future that will then have a positive impact on your long-term goals.

3. **Keep a Compelling Scoreboard.** "People play differently when they're keeping score," the 4DX authors explain. They elaborate that when attempting to drive your team's engagement toward your organization's wildly important goals, it's vital that they have a *public place to record and track their lead measures.*

4. **Create a Cadence of Accountability.** The 4DX authors conclude that the final step to help maintain a focus on lead measures is to put in place *"a rhythm of regular meetings of any team that owns a wildly important goal."*

These four disciplines are just that—disciplines. When we get to the implementation stage, our behaviors, patterns, and habits will determine our success. The 4DX framework is based on the fundamental premise that *execution is more difficult than strategizing.* Our only focus in the implementation stage is to get things done, and for everyone on our team to be accountable even if everyone just means you.

Having the habit of discipline (of applying our skills and abilities) is the wildly important task; and goals, during the implementation stage, are of paramount importance. Learning how to balance our life between our personal activities and business is a key to our success. I am not inferring that you can't have fun, or that you need to deprive yourself of time to relax. Just stay focused on your bigger overarching goals. Make it a commitment to complete your goals and reach your project vision. Give yourself a self-imposed deadline and do everything possible to reach the deadline.

Some of the distractions and behaviors are that of being a perfectionist, not knowing when to ship. *When is enough—enough?* When we focus excessive amounts of time on refining the product, we could be wasting time. Have you ever heard the phrase *just ship it?* At some point, we can't get hung up in the refinement and details any further. *We just need to ship it.*

Paralysis by analysis is close to being a perfectionist, but with one twist. If we allow ourselves to fall into the trap of analyzing every little detail, trying to save a dollar here and a dollar there through vendors and suppliers, we will drive ourselves crazy. We will spend more time attempting to save money than shipping the product. If margins are within the tolerances allowed for, then just make the decision and move forward.

Microsoft and the product Microsoft Office was originally released in the late 1980s. Bill Gates admittedly stated that he wanted the public to be his testing ground for the Office Suite of products. I can remember booting and re-booting my computer when Office was first released. The Office Suite was so buggy that the developers must have received hundreds of thousands of reports of bugs. When Microsoft released Windows 10, the word on the street was that there were lots of bugs, and many features that the consumers did not like. We, the consumers, have become the testing ground for many products, and it is our responsibility to report issues and help the organization improve the product. Our feedback is important, and so will your customers' feedback be important to your product or service.

You can't be afraid to *Just ship it*—but be certain that you have done as much "bench testing" as possible and you are 95% certain about the reliability of your product.

Recently, Samsung shipped their Galaxy Note 7 and it was a disaster. The battery in the smartphone started exploding, resulting in a complete recall of 2,000,000 smartphones. This mistake cost Samsung in excess of 2 billion dollars in lost revenue, not to mention that the consumers don't feel comfortable about the reliability of the smartphones. Product testing is a very important element, and it's a fine line on which to dance.

Influencers that Support Your Growth

Jim Rohn, a motivational speaker says, *"You are the average of the five people you spend the most time with including yourself."*

Who are you spending time with, and how are they helping you further your project, or are they distracting you from completing your goals successfully?

At implementation stage you are at a critical juncture, you need to spend time with people who are uplifting, positive, affirming, and providing you support. I know I am repeating myself, but get involved with a mastermind group or form a group yourself. Instituting a mastermind group will be the most rewarding action you can take that will assist you in developing a focus and personal mindset of follow through. You will spawn new ideas from your mastermind group. The encouragement will influence the direction of your project with a positive outcome.

I strongly recommend building a board of advisors. Your board might include your attorney, CPA, personal coach, a business owner whom you admire and has been a success. The key here is that you see the people on your advisory board as successful in your eyes. You admire them for their personal achievements and you know they can provide great advice and direction as your company grows. The size of the board should be a maximum of five and no less than three. If you choose you can offer to pay a board of director's fee. Initially, keep the fee modest—$2,500 per year or less is reasonable for a start-up company. You may even want to sweeten the deal by issuing some preferred stock in your company if you have formed a corporation. No matter what your organization formation, it is imperative to have a board of advisors. The board of advisors *are not your board of directors,* and most of the time the board of directors are stockholders, and the board of advisors are unpaid.

I've had many mentors in my life and people that I have admired who have built and run successful businesses. The first person that influenced me the most was my CPA. Robert Hoffman had his office right next door to my financial services offices when I was forming the Wanna-Be Doll Company. He was bright, articulate, fun, knowledgable, creative, and I could always count on him to have a sound solution to almost any of my challenges.

When I founded the Wanna-Be Doll Company, Bob was always there for me. He stuck by my side, unwavering during some of the most challenging times in my life. He was on my board of advisors and later became part of the board of directors with an ownership interest in the company. He also served as the CFO for Wanna-Be Doll Company. He helped in developing and crafting the private placement offering memorandum to garner the support of investors. He attended every meeting, including those in my living room where we presented the opportunity and raised funds from investors. He also supported and consoled me when I was being verbally attacked by a few of the investors who didn't like the decisions I was making regarding the strategic alliances and marketing of the Wanna-Be Dolls. It ultimately escalated to a point where the opposing parties attempted to remove me from the position of CEO. That experience could have broken even the best of business leaders, but fortunately I had the support of a mentor that I could trust and provided guidance in my deepest, darkest times.

I encourage you to find that special mentor. You need a least one person, but if you have others that is a bonus. Find a professional you admire for their business acumen, and befriend them as quickly as you can if you haven't done so already.

Strengthen Your Foundation

Daily disciplines are important in any entrepreneur's life, particularly when we are engaged in highly creative activities. I have always found it helpful to keep a morning routine. Maintaining structure in our daily activities is one of the best avenues to success. I find that stating my intentions before my feet hit the ground is critical to my day going well. Giving gratitude for what we have plays a big role as well. These two little practices have had significantly changed my perception about my personal power and the influence. Gratitude and stating intentions are simple and very powerful. Get into the practice of setting your intentions and giving gratitude. These are practices that you need to engrain in your life.

If you want to keep your sanity during your implementation stage, then start a practice of prayer, meditation, yoga, and contemplation or just sitting silently if you haven't already done so. This time of tuning in and just "being" will keep you inspired. It helps to clear your mind, and reduce the noise that impacts your mental focus— the focus that is required to stay the course.

If you don't exercise regularly, you will want to start a regular practice of keeping your body active. I am an avid cycler so I do spin classes three times per week. I start at day 6:00 a.m. with an hour yoga class, then a spin class at 7 a.m. for an hour.

No matter what your preferences, exercise is one of the practices that helps release the endorphins which reduce the chronic stress caused by the incisive drive as an entrepreneur. You will also notice that your personal stamina will increase, and you will perform at optimal levels, mentally, physically, and emotionally. Everything in your life will become easier to manage with exercise.

Eating the right foods consistently is something that I advocate. I was a vegetarian for eighteen years. Now I substitute some poultry and fish, eating a combination of foods that work for me. Having a healthy diet and eating at regular intervals is something that many entrepreneurs seem to avoid. We can get so caught up in our work, and we forget to take care of ourselves. I see so many entrepreneurs reach the implementation stage, and due to the demands on their time, they ignore their temple (the body). You can't ignore your temple. It's the vehicle for which we do our work in this world. Take care of your body, mind, and soul.

I burned the candle at both ends for so many years that it induced tremendous amounts of stress. Eating the wrong foods, and not eating at regular intervals was devastating to my blood sugar levels. I remember my energy dissipating so much that I could not focus. I was skipping meals and became so famished that I could eat the wallpaper off the walls—but in my case I defaulted to the closest cookie jar or candy dish and would eat anything in sight. When we get this super hungry, we always eat the wrong foods and our insulin levels fall and this is not a good thing. I can't emphasize it enough—take care of yourself, take time for yourself, and *enjoy* the entrepreneur journey.

We also need to consume positive content and avoid reading and listening to negative news or stories. As we personally grow and are expressing what our soul calls us to do, we can be propelled almost anywhere. The world is our oyster, what we are able to conceive and achieve is endless, but is subject to what we have programmed into our consciousness. We are only limited or benefited by *what* we have put into our consciousness, so keep feeding and filling it with unlimited possibilities and positive content.

I host a podcast program called "Inside Personal Growth." I started the program ten years ago with the intention of providing free content consisting of interviews with authors about their books. I have completed 600+ interviews with authors on personal growth, mastery, wellness, business, and spirituality. The journey has been the deepest and best education I have ever experienced. Make a practice of reading, journaling, listening to podcasts, and watching inspirational documentaries this activity spawn's great ideas. Give yourself at least thirty minutes per day to feed your soul with great inspirational content.

It's Not Business, It's Personal

Many years ago, a local magazine approached me to do a story about my coaching and consulting business. They wanted to know how I was helping small business owners grow and prosper in their businesses. I remember saying to the writer that *It's Not Business, It's Personal.* What I meant by this statement was that the journey toward meaningful work, toward making a contribution to the world, is not about our businesses. It is an inside job. The business is the vehicle that helps to carry our idea forward, but we are the fuel that makes it happen. Most of us have a car, but without the fuel, we wouldn't be propelled anywhere. The same can be said for our business.

Authenticity is a personal attribute that is quite invaluable. It means that we are real and genuine. We are not fake. We are original. Emanating an energy of authenticity is something that will propel us into the stratosphere when it comes to working with investors, customers, employees, vendors etc. People like people who are transparent and authentic. *Tell the truth; be honest and open with your employees and your customers.* If you can't do something, don't say you can, and if you can, make sure you deliver when you promise and on time.

Authenticity is a characteristic that is part of both your personal and professional life. Being authentic at home with your wife, children, and family should be natural and being authentic at work should be the same. Remember to express this wonderful attribute to everyone you meet, even if you don't know them. You might not think this is a hard thing to do but our world is filled with people trying to fake it and they don't do a very good job of it. We can spot a fake a mile away, and that's how far we should stay away from people who are faking it. Be yourself always!

The Three Vital Behaviors of Business and Personal Success

There are three additional vital behaviors of success, not including the already mentioned trait of *authenticity.*

1. **Routine & Rituals**—Having a set of routines that keep you consistent is so important to keeping your mental health. Routines help you to feel grounded, keep you focused and maintain a "normalcy" in your existence on this crazy planet. Look we all take a shower, shave, brush our teeth, eat, sleep etc. But what are the other routines that you do that are part of your everyday life? Write out your list of routines and ask

yourself which behaviors and routine serve you? The key to routines is to create them then stick to them. People without a routine flounder aimlessly. You have a purpose, vision and mission. If you are to fulfill your dreams you need to have routines.

Most people think of rituals as part of a religious practice, such as counting the rosary beads while reciting "Hail Mary's," receiving communion, bar mitzvahs, and Quinceaneras, etc. Rituals are more than just religious acts. Remember me telling you about my ritual of setting my intentions and going through my gratitude statements before allowing my feet to hit the floor in the morning? That is an example of one of my rituals. I also cite affirmations, and this is another ritual I follow in the morning.

William James, at the dawn of modern psychology argued, *"Our habits anchor us to ourselves."* As someone equally fascinated by the daily routines of artists and their curious creative rituals, and as a practitioner of both in my own life, I frequently contemplate the difference between the routine and ritual, these two supreme deities of habit. They seem to be different sides of the same coin—while routine aims to make the chaos of everyday life more containable and controllable, ritual aims to imbue the mundane with an element of the magical. No matter how you look at it, we have routines that help us get through the mundane elements of life, while the rituals help to make life more meaningful and give us that magic we need to inspire and enliven our soul."

2. **Focus & Concentration**—Nothing is more powerful than a practice of focus and concentration. Keeping the distractions to a minimum and learning how to concentrate. When you bring a new product to market it requires that you learn to

Be Here Now as Ram Dass says. Remove interruptions that can easily take you off the task at hand.

This habit of focus and concentration is one of the hardest lessons I have learned. I also believe this to be so for many other entrepreneurs. This is because of their naturally inquisitive minds. The noise from the outside world distracts creative entrepreneurs and has a tantalizing call. It is often hard to resist. We run around with a belief that the next best thing is just around the corner, or that one of those thousands of emails is going to hold the good news we have been waiting for. I have been a victim of distracting my energies into answering all those emails that I'd hope were going to bring me good fortune.

Let me tell you, don't wait for the good news through your email; *you* are your own good news. We are the ones responsible for our destiny. We are 100% responsible for what happens in our life. I know this bit of information can be hard to stomach, but it is true. You can't blame anyone else for your success or failure. You have to have the attitude that you can make it happen no matter what the circumstance.

I wish I had learned the *power of focus* at a much earlier age in my life, but no matter when you learn this amazing habit, it will be one of the single most important practices that contribute to your success.

3. **Flow and Fluidity**—When you master hacking flow you are in an altered reality.

According to positive psychologist, Mihaly Csikszentmihalyi, what you are experiencing in the moment is known as flow, a state of complete immersion in an activity. He describes the mental state of flow as *"being completely involved in an activity for its own sake. The ego falls away. Time flies. Every action, movement, and thought follows inevitably from the previous one, like playing jazz. Your whole being is involved, and you're using your skills to the utmost."*

The flow state is important in every stage of the creative process. It has been proven to accelerate our abilities to innovate. There are six factors of flow:

1. Intense and focused concentration on the present moment

2. Merging of action and awareness

3. A loss of reflective self-consciousness

4. A sense of personal control or agency over the situation or activity

5. A distortion of temporal experience

6. Experience of the activity as intrinsically rewarding, also referred to as autotelic experience.

If you are looking for more information on how to hack flow, I would recommend that you check out a website called the Flow Genome Project. This was founded by Steven Kotler the author the books *Bold, Abundance* and *The Rise of Superman*.

In a recent interview with him about *Hacking the Gap* he had this to say:

> The conscious mind can pay attention to roughly 120 bits of information at once. This is Mihaly Csikszentmihalyi's work. If 60 bits is what it takes to listen to me talk, if you're listening to two people talk at the same time,

that's it. That's the whole shebang, right? To put that in
different terms, working memory, the contents of the
conscious mind, caps out for most people at about four
items. You can at the extreme end get up to nine in your
working memory, but that's it. So if you're trying to come
up with an intuitive breakthrough or creative insight
and you have a maximum of four parts to move around,
how many great ideas do you think you're coming up
with? The subconscious, meanwhile, is extremely pre-
cise, at intrinsic processing versus extrinsic processing.
It's extremely fast, 2,000 times faster than the conscious
mind in some cases. It has unlimited RAM, literally.
When we try to figure how many different connections
the brain can make, we can't come up with them, and
we already know there are more connections in the
brain than there are stars in the sky, and it's very energy
efficient. When you trade processing in the conscious
mind to the subconscious, let the subconscious solve the
problem for you, and it pops up in your consciousness, it
certainly feels magical.

What you've got is like analog computing versus the most
powerful supercomputer that's ever been built.

One of the things that I've learned as I've gotten older as a creative is you can't actually be a creative, whatever the field, without
breakthroughs, the kind that really require intuition. You can
muscle through the creative process and just sweat through it. But
there are huge structural problems, when things have to get moved
around in really macroscopic ways. I think the same thing happens
in science discovery and technology discovery. You need those
intuitive insights because there are just too many variables. The
conscious mind can't process it.

Turning Strategy into Action

Strategy is nothing but a good intention until we take action to implement and execute on our plan.

To move into action, we must define at least three but no more than five action areas or initiatives that are going to help launch your product. Most start-up organizations don't have the resources to focus on more than three initiatives at any one time. Once you have defined the three important initiatives, then define the tasks that need to be performed to execute on the initiatives. Assign a reasonable timeline for completion and assign a champion to assist in getting the tasks completed.

> **Who is going to be accountable for driving the initiative and successful completion of that particular initiative and associated tasks?**
>
> **Do you have a vision for success?**
>
> **What does it look and feel like?**
>
> **What measurable do you want to achieve?**

If you can paint a clear vision in your mind's eye about what success looks and feels like then you have won the battle.

Ed Morrison, the director of Purdue Agile Strategy Lab, says *"That one needs to commit to a 30-day review process, where you periodically make adjustments to your plan."*

A strategic plan is a fluid document, always in motion. Things will change and we need to remain fluid and open to change.

I conduct strategic planning meetings with my clients and we have developed something called the *Hacking the Gap Matrix.* These eight-hour meetings with the leadership team are usually broken up into two four-(4) hour segments. The purpose is to guide the leadership of the organization in defining their vision, mission, purpose, and BHAG (Big Hairy Audacious Goals). The matrix is so much more than an excel spreadsheet with initiatives, goals, and tasks defined. It is a process of inclusion where everyone on the leadership team buys into the vision, initiatives, and goals. Once you have buy-in, you have lift off because everyone is committed.

When leadership uses an inclusionary strategy planning happens, and the teams are aware that the founder/CEO is committed to improving the company culture. He or she is focused on inclusion and meeting the needs of everyone so that they can lift the organization to a new level of employee engagement. The leadership and employees are excited about the new direction and appreciate being part of that *unified vision.*

WHAT ARE YOUR VERY IMPORTANT COMPANY-WIDE INITIATIVES? WHO IS RESPONSIBLE FOR DRIVING THEM TO COMPLETION?

The *Hacking the Gap Matrix* process turns strategy into action, it gets people moving and things accomplished at speeds not previously experienced before inside the organizations.

When mastering the process of *Hacking the Gap*, we are looking for every advantage possible. When we take the time to invest into a process like the *Hacking the Gap Matrix*, we will find that it is like rocket fuel. People and resources become available for projects and initiatives that we only once dreamed of doing, but were fearful that it would concentrate the workload on employees that would result in burnout. No need to worry about burnout, everyone will be sharing in the workload and enjoying the new found teamwork.

When we are *Hacking the Gap*, we are finding the shortest distance between two points with the least amount of resistance while applying our highest human potential and growing as human beings. When you bring bright engaged minds together, a synergy and synchronicity is created resulting in huge exponential growth and development for everyone.

If the cycle from intuition to implementation is shortened, your company saves money—the employees are happier, and you are less stressed. There is not an entrepreneur or business owner reading this book that doesn't have an interest in improving efficiencies, reducing mistakes, finding engaged employees, and keeping customers satisfied through the launch of any product or service.

If you identify and apply your resources to *Hacking the Gap*, you will find that all of these game-changing breakthroughs and benefits are available and waiting for you. Give your leadership team and employees the freedom to *Hack the Gap* by finding ways to improve performance through ideas that shorten product development cycles while still keeping your strict standards of quality.

We all want to *Hack the Gap*, and we need to trust that there are many avenues that are available in reaching our goals and vision. It doesn't have to be a struggle. It can easy, fun, exciting and we can make money at the same time. Don't buy into a story of struggle. That's the story of non-believers and those individuals don't have faith in their own dreams.

Mindset Applications for Hacking the Gap Toward Actions & Accountability

We are all looking for ways to decrease the time and energy on any of our projects. These tips on actions and accountability will assist you:

- Take one full day per week to become a recluse and do the deep work.

- Focus on the four (4) disciplines of execution: 1. Focus on the wildly important. 2. Act on lead measures. 3. Keep a compelling scorecard. 4. Create a cadence of accountability.

- Always be authentic to yourself and others.

- Have daily routines and rituals that support your personal performance and mental health.

- "Be Here Now." Stay focused and concentrate on solving problems and creating new opportunities. Focus on looking for the opportunity.

- You cannot force flow, but you can create the environment and circumstances that allow it to occur more often. Create the type of environment that fosters your attaining a flow state where there is a merging of action and awareness.

- Hire someone to help facilitate a Matrix for your organization. This single step will propel initiatives forward and get projects completed like no other activity you could invest your time and money into.

- Define the purpose, vision, and BHAG for your organization. Check to make sure that it aligns with your personal vision and goals.

- Know that the whole is greater than the sum of the parts. Encourage team participation and inclusion to develop ideas, solve problems and create fully satisfied customers/clients.

- Don't buy into your struggle story. Rewrite it with a story filled with synchronicity, collaboration, fun, and happiness.

Conclusion

The time you've spent reading this book has been a journey we have taken together—from accessing your intuition to implementation of your special product, service, or project. I endeavored to inspire and encourage you to take risks and become alive with enthusiasm about your ideas, and hopefully I was successful in doing just that.

If you are going to take away anything from this book, I hope that it will be that you are capable of breaking old patterns of behavior and limiting thoughts that have held you back from truly exploring and doing what you want to do. Learning how to listen to your intuition is a special gift, and I trust that I have provided you with some new techniques to approaching the process. I also know that having more insights in your life is a direct result of you opening up the pathways of your consciousness and looking for the possibilities. Our lives offer endless decision, choices, and possibilities. We never know when that person or circumstance and/or event in our life will bring together the perfect storm to help create, develop, or invent something special.

Remember—no idea is a bad idea. You just might need to refine it and work out the kinks. Recording your ideas is a must. Please keep an idea journal in a place where you can write down your great ideas. The timing for the development might not be immediate, but if you keep revisiting the idea you will know when to jump into action. It takes the inspiration to spark your desire to move forward.

Accessing your desire and inspiration is when you have a "knowing" that it is time to start developing, marketing, testing, researching that special idea. Believe me you will "know" when the time is right. You will receive signs, symbols, and synchronicities that indicate that *now* is the time. And you will be met with resistance—it is a given. Please do not fall into its trap—it is easy to do. When you feel the urge to be distracted and see yourself getting off track, fight the feelings and apply your gifts and talents into the idea that you desire to manifest into physical form.

Incubation is that stage of the *Hacking the Gap* process where you get to apply your skills and abilities in testing and manifesting your idea. Have fun, play, and engage your mind to the successful development of your idea. If you have gotten this far in the process, chances are that you are going to make it to the finish line. This stage of development might include an investment, so no matter how you get the investment, please don't run out of the funding you need to complete your idea. I encourage you to anticipate your funding needs. Many great projects are thwarted because the inventor ran out of funds and became discouraged and never completed the development of his or her idea.

It can be a long journey from intuition to innovation. It requires that you understand how much of your energy is going to be required to see your project to completion. Keep in mind that you need to take care of yourself first and foremost. Take time to exercise, meditate, journal, commune with nature, vacation—whatever you need to do to balance your life. If you take care of your physical body, the process of developing your idea into a successful product or service will be much easier. Not only will you have more energy, accessing the brain power required to think about and put all the pieces together will flow more easily and naturally. This step in the *Hacking the Gap* process is not one of the steps to be glossed over or taken lightly. Keeping a healthy body, mind, and soul is paramount to your succeeding. Each day give gratitude for what you have, and set your intentions. This practice will make a big difference to you managing your energy. Divide your to-do list into meaningful, mandatory, and mundane. Spend the first two hours of your day working on the meaningful to-dos. This practice will also help with your energy management. Attempt to keep out of self-judgment, attachment, and resistance. These three emotions and feelings will drain your energy and are a waste of your valuable time.

After you have developed the prototype or you have refined the business plan around your service you want to develop, you now get to innovate. You might think that the innovation process is complete, but far from it. You have to test, and re-test your idea with your prospective customers. You might find that you need to revise, revisit, or refine elements of your product or service. Bench testing your product is just one phase of the testing. You want to have a small group of testers really put your product through the ringer. You will find out what else needs to be fixed or refined to improve your product. This same process applies for the development of a service as well. Get a group of people to test your service and provide you with feedback no matter what the service, then make alterations accordingly.

You are now ready to make the next major step in the development and delivery of your product or service—implementation. This can be the most taxing of all of the steps, and requires tremendous focus and dedication to finding the correct channels to market and sell your idea. This step is all about growing your business and exploring the partnerships, relationships, and opportunities to get traction with your product or service. Keep a focus on what is wildly important, act on lead measures, keep a compelling score card, and create a cadence of accountability within your business or for yourself.

This stage in the *Hacking the Gap* process requires that you maintain your diligence, focus, and fortitude. Take the time to re-define your vision and purpose for "why" you started the development of your idea. Along the way it can be easy to get so focused on the development, that we lose sight of the "why" we are doing what we initially intended to do. Always know your "why" and your purpose—these are you guiding lights, and they ground you. They allow you to access your soul and listen to that powerful intuition which has been with you throughout the project, but you might not have accessed as frequently as you would have liked.

When you come to the end of something, it is just the beginning of another step. In the implementation stage you are not at the end, you really are at the beginning. You are birthing your idea to the world. This is an exciting time and it's filled with tasks and to-dos that can easily become overwhelming. Hopefully, by this stage you have been able to hire others to assist you, but if not remember, you have tremendous opportunity to gain the traction for your idea by just showing your product and telling your story. You never know what might happen. The right person just might come along who wants to help you market, sell, and get distribution for your product or service. There are lots of people that don't want to go through the *Hacking the Gap* process, yet are great at marketing and sales. This is the time to identify and team up with them.

I hope you have enjoyed *Hacking the Gap* and have learned new ideas and practices that will change your life for the better. Below is a recap of the listing of the Mindset Applications per chapter. It's my intention that these ideas and practices will help you at learning how to *Hack the Gap.*

Mindset Applications for Hacking the Gap to Developing the Voice of Intuition

- Spend more time in contemplation and silence. This could be mindfulness practices or meditation both in the morning and evening.

- When working on your computer make sure that you give yourself breaks of about fifteen minutes every hour. You might be saying "really!" Yes, really. You need to get away from the screen to reset your mind and treat yourself to a break.

- Take more time to be in nature. Taking walks on the beach or in the woods is great. But if this is not possible just head to a park or somewhere you can commune with nature. Richard Louv, author of *The Nature Principle*, says, "Reconnecting to the natural world is fundamental to human health, well-being, spirit, and survival."

- Write in your journal for fifteen minutes, three times per week or when you are called to make an entry about something that is meaningful, or an observation you had. Keep it handy or use a digital version such as Penzu (penzu.com).

- Exercise, take yoga classes, tai chi, or anything that gets your body moving. I encourage regular exercise for 60–90 minutes at least three times per week. No matter what you do, just get your body moving. Amazing things happen, including the release of wonderful chemicals into your bloodstream that move you into an altered state of consciousness.

- Pamper yourself. Get a massage, a pedicure, take a sauna. Treat yourself with the ultimate amount of respect and self-care.

- Spend time with friends and family. Community is important. And if you want inspiration and support for your business, join a mastermind group where you can be supported. However, be cautious about the amount of time you spend with others, and make sure the values of those in the groups you spend time with are aligned with your own. American entrepreneur and motivational speaker, Jim Rohn, said, "We are the average of the five people we spend the most time with." Choose wisely.

- Find a charitable cause to support that is aligned with your values and donate time and money to the cause. There is nothing better than giving back to the community you live in or to a cause that has an effect worldwide. No matter what you do get involved in some way.

- If you don't have a hobby, find one. Play a musical instrument, sing, knit, do crossword puzzles, read, write... anything that activates your mind and keeps you focused—that isn't work related.

- Practice gratitude. Daily write at least three things for which you are grateful for... your health, your family, your opportunities, etc.

Mindset Applications for Hacking the Gap of Insight & Aha Moments

- Create affirmations that are positive and have a future vision. Write the affirmation and post them where you can read them often. I recommend that you reinforce the affirmation daily if possible by citing them aloud. Here's an example: *I am enjoying spreading the message of Hacking the Gap around the world.*

- Read books on topics that you believe will help you foster ideas and insight moments. There are millions of books published worldwide and found on Amazon, Barnes and Noble, Indi Books, and more—either paper or digital. Order or download something that is out of your wheelhouse, outside your norm, and see how you feel reading it. Stretching the base of your beliefs and ideas is a good thing. (See a recommended list at the back of the book)

- Listen to podcasts on a regular basis. Podcasts that assist you in expanding your mind and getting you thinking in a new way. I created a program called *Inside Personal Growth* and have been interviewing authors on topics of personal growth, wellness, business, mastery, and spirituality for over ten years. Go to www.insidepersonalgrowth.com to listen to some of the over 600+ podcasts.

- Imagine if a video camera was following you for the day. Capture your observations of your actions in your journal and review what you wrote. Ask yourself if you like what you did during the day. What might you change or alter to make your day more enjoyable? Did you meet and interact with the people you wanted to?

- Certainly attempt to find reflection time or meditation time in your day, preferably morning and evening.

- Turn off the television or electronic devices at least one-hour prior to retiring to bed for a restful evening.

- Keep a note pad by your bedside. Insights and ideas that manifest don't have a time clock, and I know you will be awakened with ideas you will want to capture. Please capture them no matter how crazy they might seem. Trust your Crazy Ideas. They often disappear if we go back to sleep without writing them down.

- Relax and unwind. It's not a privilege; it's a necessity to stay balanced, stress-free, and open to new insights. This could be an evening walk, a yoga class or anything that you enjoy doing that alters your mind into a relaxed state of consciousness.

- Remember to plan your day with periodic breaks. As author Terry Hershey says, there is power in the pause. Schedule space between your meetings to regroup and prepare for the next item on your calendar. Provide yourself with time to reflect on previous meetings, maybe even writing up notes on your thoughts.

Mindset Applications to Hack the Gap of Frequency/Recording and Capturing Your Ideas

The following is a short list of ways you can invoke *Hacking the Gap* to sustain the flow of ideas:

- Always keep a paper and pencil with you or by your bedside. You need to be able to record ideas that come to you.

- Practice the *Silence Solution* which is a daily practice of giving yourself thirty minutes to practice the eight steps outlined above in this chapter.

- Do "Brain Dumps" frequently. Brain dumps can be done anytime, but are especially effective before entering the *Silence Solution* sessions. Getting in the habit of doing "Brain Dumps" is a good habit of keeping your mind clear, allowing you to access to your intuition at any time.

- The world is always calling you and distracting you from being in silence. Turn off electronic devices, smart phones, radio, television, and computers. Take a break one day a week if that is possible. Believe me people can wait. There is nothing so important that you can't take a "retreat day" from the phones and emails.

- Learn to take cues from nature and your surrounds. Look for signs, that you are on the right track (or perhaps off track). They are all around. Interpret the meaning of those signs. You are being guided at all times by the Universe. By deciphering the code of a soaring hawk or the appearance of a dolphin close to shore, you may be that much closer to *Hacking the Gap* of your brilliance.

- Do whatever you need to do to eliminate stress in your life. Stress is the single biggest killer of great ideas. Exercise, meditate, listen to music—whatever you need to or "not do" to remove the stress.

Mindset Applications for Hacking the Gap of Inspiration

- If you listen to music, then listen to more. Nothing can be quite as inspiring as jamming to your favorite tunes. Let the music take you to another world, one where you are released from all your cares and obligations.

- Practice doing brain dumps of all that stuff that is in your head. Use this application to get your "to-dos" out of your RAM (random accessory memory) and on to paper. You cannot do anything if you're just thinking about your to-dos. They all require action and that likely requires that you write an email, make a phone call, or set up a meeting. No matter what it is, don't let it take up the creative space in your consciousness.

- Who is the most inspiring person you know? Write down their name. (Your mother, father, Gandhi, whomever.) If you can speak with them, then call immediately. If it is someone famous and you don't believe you can reach them or they are dead, then listen to a podcast, video, or whatever they have created that inspires you. The key is to soak your consciousness with their essence so that you are so inspired you take action.

- Are you part of a mastermind group, or any group of like-minded people that give you inspiration? If not join one, or create a group of your own if you are not part of a group. Being in community is a must; you can't go the creative process alone. 1 + 1 = 3. There is amazing synergy from the process of sharing your ideas, thoughts, and challenges with others that care and want to help you become successful.

- I am not certain where you are in the development cycle of your idea, product, or service, but taking time to "chill" is always a great way to get inspired. Commune with nature. Get away from your work and take a break. Plan at least three days away from your office and your day-to-day responsibilities every quarter to rejuvenate and reset. You will find that this "away time" will get your engines reengaged and inspired ideas and breakthroughs will occur much more quickly. This is one of the best ways to assist you in *"Hacking the Gap."*

Mindset Applications for Hacking the Gap of Incubation and the Evolution of Your Insights, Ideas, and Inspirations

- Research your idea thoroughly. Spend time looking into your competition in the market, and know what problem you are solving for your customers and why they might want something like your new product or service.

- Know who is going to consume your service or product. Who is your avatar and what makes them tick?

- Give presentations to people once you have your idea fully developed. Spend this time getting prospective customer feedback and gathering information that could make your product or service better.

- Once you have gathered the data look inside yourself and listen to your soul's voice. What ideas will make your idea better, and only focus on those. Remember you will not be all things to all people, and there is no need to try.

- Try if possible to keep things simple. Some of the simplest ideas have made millions of dollars. Post-it notes over $29 billion in sales. Sara Blakely's Spanx undergarment for women, has made her a billionaire. Snuggie blanket has sold over 30 million.

- Some of your best ideas will spring out of "connecting the dots." Make sure you allow yourself the space and time to get in the "connecting the dots" space. Take more time to sit and think, and remember to do it in silence if possible.

- Many ideas are just more improved products or services of an existing product or service. What have you noticed that you believe needs changing or improving, and why? Ask your friends for feedback on your ideas.

- Think about who you might need to help you develop this new product or service. Are you going to need a prototype, if so who do you know who has the proper equipment to make it? Do you have a drawing or plan for the product? If so, share this with people that prototype new products.

- Have you thought about how much money will be required to develop your product or service? Do you have the money or are you going to need investors in your idea? Think through who might be your best investor(s) and why? What are their passions and do they align with your new product or service?

- Pull all the pieces of the development of your idea together, and think through every step of the development process. This is where the project management software will come in handy. Keep asking questions of everyone involved in the project, from vendors to friends and family. And again, solicit feedback as you progress with the development.

Mindset Applications for Hacking the Gap for Better Living

The following are my prescriptions for *Hacking the Gap* for a better life. Remember the key to any prescription is to follow the advice.

- Set intentions and give gratitude upon waking up in the morning.

- Remove judgment for others and self-judgment from your thinking. This requires work and reminding yourself that you are in the process—and judgment is highly detrimental to a better life.

- Set goals with soul and don't fill up your day with a list of to-dos without meaning and that are not aligned with your values and purpose.

- Try the technique of dividing your goals into three categories: meaningful, mandatory and mundane. Work first thing in the morning on meaningful goals and you will find that your daily focus changes for the good.

- Take the time to define your values and purpose in life, and learn to live by them.

- Give back; find something that you are passionate about—a cause, charity or personal passion; give the gift of time, money or in whatever way possible.

- Develop a mastermind group, or meet with associates or like-minded friends. The goal here is to be supported and challenged at the same time. This is a definite must if you want to grow and have a more meaningful life.

- Read something positive daily—a book, blog, article, or quotes. If you are trying to stimulate your creativity and connect new neuro-pathways. The science recommends reading something that is opposite of what you normally read. So if you read personal growth books all the time, try reading a novel.

- Stay away from the negative news. We are bombarded with immediate news from our cell phones, TV, Internet, iPads, and this can be a real downer. If you need to know do it quickly and only once per day.

- Write positive affirmation(s) or mantra and keep them in front of your computer or on a 3x5 cards and carry them with you throughout the day.

- Give yourself breaks from your work. Take a walk, commune with nature, exercise. Whatever you do, take a pause. It has been proven that we reach a point of satiation and our minds need a break from the computer or whatever we are working on.

Mindset Applications for Hacking the Gap of Innovation

If you want to *Hack the Gap* toward better innovations, I have some simple mindset applications that you can make part of your life, and hopefully this will make things easier for you.

If you practice these applications as part of your habits and routines, you will find that it is making the process of stepping into innovating easier and more fun.

- Innovating a new product is hard work. Don't forget to do the little things and put "X" on your calendar to remind yourself of your win along the way.

- Self-judgment is your nemesis; remind yourself that you are on purpose. Read your purpose statement and affirmations daily. Create a mantra for those times you begin to doubt yourself. *I can do anything one day at a time.*

- Do not get attached to the outcome of what you believe is the "right" way. There are many paths up the mountain, and they all lead to the same destination.

- Resistance is futile. Stay in the flow of life by being open. Collaborate with others. Ask for advice and take it all in but only be influenced by what serves you and moves the projects forward.

- Broaden your perspective and open up to the window to the world. Read, listen, observe, and look for signposts. The more you can do this the quicker your idea will be manifest into reality.

- You are on a journey both personally and professionally. Your personal and spiritual growth is happening as a result of your willingness to take on this project. Enjoy the journey—journal your experience and read what you have written. Your entries will amaze you.

- Become an Essentialist in the process of your journey. Remove all the unnecessary distractions and focus your attention on the one single thing—the development of your product or service. A good daily practice would be to write out the essential and necessary things to accomplish, not the mundane and meaningless. Focus, concentrate, and apply your critical thinking skills.

- Eliminate time constraints that cause you stress. While you might have an unlimited budget to bring your product or service to market, stressing yourself out over time will only make it worse—and you will make more mistakes. Remove clocks, cell phones, and any reference to time when you sit down to work on your project. You will find that "time" flies.

- Start your day with quiet time, reflection, or meditation. Give yourself at least fifteen minutes. After you have done this practice, write down the immediate thoughts or ideas that come into your mind after your meditation. Scan those ideas to see if they have any relevance to your core idea, and the development of your product or service.

Mindset Applications for Hacking the Gap Toward Actions & Accountability

We are all looking for ways to decrease the time and energy on any of our projects. These tips on actions and accountability will assist you:

- Take one full day per week to become a recluse and do the deep work.

- Focus on the four (4) disciplines of execution: 1. Focus on the wildly important. 2. Act on lead measures. 3, Keep a compelling scorecard. 4. Create a cadence of accountability.

- Always be authentic to yourself and others.

- Have daily routines and rituals that support your personal performance and mental health.

- "Be Here Now." Stay focused and concentrate on solving problems and creating new opportunities. Focus on looking for the opportunity.

- You cannot force flow, but you can create the environment and circumstances that allow it to occur more often. Create the type of environment that fosters your attaining a flow state where there is a merging of action and awareness.

- Hire someone to help facilitate a Matrix for your organization. This single step will propel initiatives forward and get projects completed like no other activity you could invest your time and money into.

- Define the purpose, vision, and BHAG for your organization. Check to make sure that it aligns with your personal vision and goals.

- Know that the whole is greater than the sum of the parts. Encourage team participation and inclusion to develop ideas, solve problems and create fully satisfied customers/clients.

- Don't buy into your struggle story. Rewrite it with a story filled with synchronicity, collaboration, fun, and happiness.

References

Books

Allen, David. *Making it all Work: Winning at the Game of Work and the Business of Life*. New York: Penguin, 2009.

Barnett Bain *The Book of Doing and Being: Rediscovering Creativity in Life, Love, and Work*. New York: Atria Books, 2015.

Belitz, Charlene and Meg Lundstrom. *The Power of Flow: Practical Ways to Transform Your Life with Meaningful Coincidence*. New York: Harmony, 1998.

Davis, Josh. *Two Awesome Hours-Science-Based Strategies to Harness Your Best Time and Get Your Most Important Work Done*. New York: HarperOne. 2015.

Diamandis, Peter and Kotler Stephen. *Abundance: The Future is Better Than You Think*. New York: Free Press, 2012.

Draft, Richard L. *The Executive and the Elephant: A Leader's Guide to Building Inner Excellence*. Hoboken: Jossey-Bass, 2010.

Gazzaley, Adam and Larry D. Rosen, *The Distracted Mind: Ancient Brains in a High Tech World*. Cambridge: The MIT Press, 2016.

Gilbert, Elizabeth. *Big Magic: Creative Living Beyond Fear*. New York: Riverhead Books, 2015.

Gladwell, Malcolm. *Outliers: The Story of Success*. Boston: Back Bay Books, 2011.

Gordon, MD, James. *Unstuck-Your Guide to the Seven-Stage Journey Out of Depression*. New York: Penguin, 2009.

Katie, Byron and Stephen Mitchell. *Loving What Is: Four Questions that Can Change Your Life*. New York: Three Rivers Press, 2003.

Langshur, Eric and Nate Klemp. *Start Here: Master the Lifelong Habit of Wellbeing*. New York: North Star Way, 2016.

Loehr, Jim and Tony Schwartz. *The Power of Full Engagement: Managing Energy, Not Time is the Key to High Performance and Personal Renewal*. New York: Free Press, 2003.

Louv, Richard. *The Nature Principle: Reconnecting with Life in a Virtual Age*. Chapel Hill: Algonquin Books, 2012.

Maraboli, Steve. *Life, the Truth, and Being Free*. CreateSpace Independent Publishing Platform, 2014.

McCarthy, Kevin. *The On Purpose Person, Making Your Life Make Sense*. Irving: On Purpose Publishing, 2013.

McChesney, Chris, Sean Covey, and Jim Huling. *The 4 Discipline of Execution: Achieving Your Wildly Important Dreams*. New York: Free Press, 2012.

McKeown, Greg. *Essentialism: The Disciplined Pursuit of Less*. New York: Crown Business, 2014.

Moss, Robert. *Sidewalk Oracles: Playing with Signs, Symbols, and Synchronicity in Everyday Life*. Novata: New World Library, 2015.

Nepo, Mike. *The One Life We're Given: Finding the Wisdom That Waits in Your Heart*. New York: Atria Books, 2016.

Newport, Cal. *Deep Work: Rules for Focused Success in a Distracted World*. New York: Grand Central Publishing, 2016.

Orloff, Judith. *Second Sight: An Intuitive Psychiatrist Tells Her Extraordinary Story and Shows You How to Tap Your Own Inner Wisdom*. New York: Three Rivers Press, 2010.

Pressfield, Steven. *The War of Art: Break Through the Blocks and Win Your Inner Creative Battles*. Los Angeles: Black Irish Entertainment, 2012.

Robbins, Tony. *Awaken the Giant Within: How to Take Immediate Control of Your Mental, Emotional, Physical and Financial Destiny!* New York: Free Press, 1992.

Spinelli, Jr. Stephen and Heather McGowan. *Disrupt Together How Teams Consistently Innovate*. Indianapolis: Pearson FT Press, 2013.

Warren, Rick. *The Purpose Driven Life: What on Earth Am I Here For?* Grand Rapids: Zondervan, 2013.

Weiner, Eric. *The Geography of Genius: A Search for the World's Most Creative Places From Ancient Athens to Silicon Valley*. New York, Simon and Schuster, 2016.

Whyte, David. *Crossing the Unknown Sea: Work as a Pilgrimage of Identity.* Riverhead, 2002. New York: Riverhead Books, 2002.

Willard, Jill. *Intuitive Being: Connect with Spirit, Find Your Center, and Choose an Intentional Life.* New York: HarperElixer, 2016.

Blogs & Magazines

Hamilton, Michelle. "TK" Runners World. [day May 2013.]

Reid, Glenn. "What It's Really Like Working with Steve Jobs." October 12, 2011. http://inventor-labs.com/blog/2011/10/12/what-its-really-like-working-with-steve-jobs.html. Accessed, January 15, 2017.

Podcasts

Inside Personal Growth: www.insidepersonalgrowth.com

Products, Apps, and Software

Goalscape—for setting and tracking goals. (www.goalscape.com)

Evernote for my entire note taking, and I find it quite efficient and useful. (www.evernote.com)

iMindMap9—for mind mapping

Mind Meister—for mind mapping

Penzu (penzu.com)—for journaling

Rev Voice Recorder. (www.rev.com)

Project Management Software

Asana (www.asana.com)

Basecamp (www.basecamp.com)

Dapulse (www.dapulse.com)

Wizeline (www.wizeline.com)

Greg Voisen,
Author and Speaker and Entrepreneur

Greg Voisen is a thought leader in the personal growth and human potential movement. Founder of Inside Personal Growth, Greg has interviewed via podcasts over 630+ authors and has developed over 900 hours of recorded podcasts over the last 10 years. Topics include personal growth, business, wellness, mastery, and spirituality. http://www.insidepersonalgrowth.com

Greg's primary focus is advising small-to-medium-size business owners on financial management, human capital development, process improvement, and sales and marketing. His company eLuminate, Inc. has a team of six associates dedicated to fulfilling the needs of his clients. You can learn more about eLuminate, Inc. at www.eluminate.net or www.hackingthegap.com.

Greg is also co-author with John Selby of *Wisdom, Wellness and Redefining Work*, which is designed to bring awareness to businesses about the impacts of stress in the workplace and to effect a positive change in coping with stress, reducing medical costs, and improving employee's overall engagement and performance.

Greg has a bachelor's degree in Business Management from San Diego State University, and a Master's Degree in Spiritual Psychology from the University of Santa Monica.

To learn more about Greg's entrepreneurial endeavors, go to www.hackingthegap.com/gregvoisen to get a full list of his experience and background.

He lives in Encinitas, CA with his wife Lisa and their two dogs Buster and Juno.

CPSIA information can be obtained
at www.ICGtesting.com
Printed in the USA
FSHW04n1035080318
45225FS